James Granville Adderley

Stephen Remarx

The Story of a Venture in Ethics

James Granville Adderley

Stephen Remarx
The Story of a Venture in Ethics

ISBN/EAN: 9783744748490

Printed in Europe, USA, Canada, Australia, Japan

Cover: Foto ©Thomas Meinert / pixelio.de

More available books at **www.hansebooks.com**

STEPHEN REMARX

*THE STORY OF A VENTURE
IN ETHICS*

BY

JAMES ADDERLEY

παρὰ Θεῷ πάντα δυνατὰ ἐστι

NEW EDITION

LONDON
EDWARD ARNOLD
37 BEDFORD STREET, STRAND
Publisher to the India Office
1893

CONTENTS

Chap.		Page
I.	Stephen	1
II.	Hoxton	7
III.	A Lecture	21
IV.	Westward Ho!	38
V.	The Docker	46
VI.	In the Wilderness	56
VII.	Conversion	66
VIII.	In Excelsis	78
IX.	The Venture	96
X.	Some Pastoral Epistles	111
XI.	Progress	116
XII.	Judgment	129
XIII.	On the Feast of Stephen	140

STEPHEN REMARX

I

STEPHEN

STEPHEN REMARX was an orphan, the son of the late Lord Remarx of Balustrade Abbey in Surrey. His brother, Lord Remarx, had passed into another sphere, where the wicked do not cease from troubling and the weary are not at rest; he had, in fact, "gone to the bad." Gambling had done it. The estate was ruined, his wife had left him, his three boys had gone away from home, the eldest to Manitoba, the second to Madras and the youngest—well, nobody knew of his whereabouts. He was last seen, when he was "sacked" from Eton for catapulting a master's wife on her way to chapel. Lord Remarx spent a good deal of his time at Monte Carlo, but occasionally came to London to vote for the Deceased Wife's Sister's Bill or to have a tooth out. But he never came to his brother's church, the fashionable Church of St. Mark and the Angels, Chelsea. This was not surprising, for the two brothers were quite different from one another.

In the old days at Balustrade when boys they had never agreed. Stephen was for ever reading books, while his brother was bird's-nesting. On a Sunday afternoon, while the elder son was smoking in the hayloft, Stephen would love to sit in the garden with his mother, and listen to her while she taught him the Catechism in her old-fashioned way. "Who are my betters?" the boy would ask. "Well, my dear," the Countess would reply, "you have not many of them, that part of the Catechism is written for the lower orders: in fact, you are yourself a 'better' and they must order themselves lowly and reverently to you." "I see," said Stephen, though he felt somehow that his mother was wrong.

Not long after this his parents died, and he was left very much to himself, his old guardian and uncle, the Marquis of St. Alphege, having a theory that the more you interfered with a boy the worse he became. If this theory were correct, the young Earl Remarx would have been a terrible villain, if the Marquis had paid any attention to his education. As it was he went quite fast enough on the downward path. At twenty-one he married an actress from the Jollity Theatre, whose chief accomplishment was a peculiar twist of her ankles in the dance between the verses of a comic song; at twenty-four he had nearly been put into prison at Bordeaux for stealing somebody's pearl studs; and at twenty-six he had run through so much money, that her ladyship thought he was not worth hanging on to, and so went back to the Jollity, where she is still performing nightly. Stephen on the other hand went on quietly. At Eton he was chiefly known as a "beastly sap," which translated into more elegant and Christian language means that he tried to construe his Homer without the aid of a translation, and to gather a little of the knowledge and training which a Public School is in theory supposed to supply. He was a good cricketer, and would have been in the eleven had he not foolishly persisted in reading for a Scholarship in the summer half. He was also partially disabled by a sprain, caused in carrying home the Captain of the Boats drunk on the Fourth of June. If it were asked what good did Eton do to him, the answer would be found in that peculiar charm of real gentility and in that high sense of honour which characterized him all through his life.

Oxford was, however, a more congenial sphere for Stephen Remarx. He made there the acquaintance of several first-rate men of a lower class. Most of them had been educated at country Grammar Schools, but they had the manners of gentlemen all the same. They thought it a good thing to read hard and to row hard, and somehow they had a very happy time. It is true they scarcely ever went to wines, and never let off fireworks under the Dean's nose, nor broke the Chapel windows, nor ducked the porter in the fountain; but, nevertheless, they appeared to be quite as well bred as the Duke of Lundy's two sons, or the young Marquis of Lindisfarne who did all these things regularly every term. Stephen was also a favourite with many of the tutors and senior men. He was a particular friend of Frederick Hope, whose theological lectures created so deep an impression on the Oxford of that time. But it was not at the lectures chiefly that Stephen got at the mind of this remarkable clergyman. It was in the quiet talks they had together at night in Hope's rooms. Then it was, that as Hope murmured on over the fire for hours together of religion and social problems, there grew up in Stephen's mind an ideal, the realisation of which has caused his story to be written.

In later times, when Stephen became a much talked of man, he would always say to young men who came and spoke to him:

"I should never have done what I have done nor been what I have been if it had not been for Frederick Hope. It was he who opened my eyes, it was he who made me first wonder whether God really meant great crowds of men to live in poverty and overwork, while many live in luxury and idleness upon the labours of the rest: it was he who made me look round about me at the undergraduates of my College, rich young men wasting their time, throwing away the priceless opportunities of Oxford, which many poor men would give their very eyes to have, but which are denied them, because, forsooth, they have not enough money to pay for a university career: aye, and it was he," Stephen would say, "who pointed me to the One True Liberator, who made me feel certain that if ever a brighter day should come for England, and if ever a way out of the darkness should be found, it would be through Christ."

II

HOXTON

STEPHEN was ordained by the Bishop of London, and received a title from the Rev. David Bloose, D.D., Vicar of St. Titus, Hoxton. Dr. Bloose had been a distinguished person in his day, but his day was now over. He had rowed stroke of his college eight in the year 1854, he had won a Scholarship, he had edited a play of Aristophanes, he had maintained a healthy opposition to all the various theological bugbears of the century, "Essays and Reviews," "Ecce Homo," "Robert Elsmere" and "Lux Mundi:" he believed intensely in himself, wrote various pamphlets which he gave away to his friends and to his housemaid, and belonged to the National Club. His grateful College could hardly have done less than they did, when they appointed this distinguished Son of theirs to the parish of St. Titus, the plum of their East-end patronage with a Church-rate producing £700 a year. Dr Bloose readily exchanged his country vicarage at Slumberside for this exciting sphere of labour in Hoxton. Not that he had any intention of allowing himself to be excited or to be afflicted with an increase of labour. Labour, indeed! Why, already he was spending four hours a day in writing books or correcting proofs, two hours were devoted to his sofa, for his doctor had ordered it as necessary for his health, four more hours were for exercise, two for recreative reading, three for meals, and the rest for bed. What more could he do? So he settled himself at the Vicarage of St. Titus. He had been there twenty years when Stephen was ordained. During that time he had preached some two thousand sermons, and had combated nearly every modern heresy from Agnosticism to Theosophy for the edification of the verger, the two pew-openers, fifteen old men and fifteen old women, who, by the charity of Dame Alice Daw, ob. A.D. 1764, were given three pence a-piece and a loaf every Sunday morning, and double the amount on Christmas Day.

He did not visit the sick, because he had a tendency to faint away if the walls of the room, in which he might happen to be, were less than fourteen feet high. He seldom rubbed up against his parishioners, for fear of receiving from them an addition to the liveliness of his person. He had once during a sermon seen what he at first thought was a Protestant miracle: one of the ink-blots on his manuscript began to move across the page as if on legs. Suddenly realising that it was no blot, but one of those marvels of the Universe which owe more for the pleasure of existence to the carelessness of man than to the care of the Creator, the good Doctor turned a deadly white, and regardless of the fact that he was in the midst of convincing his little flock of the absurdities of Pantheism, he fled down the pulpit stairs, and gathering up the skirts of his Geneva gown raced down the aisle and into the Vicarage nearly knocking over Mrs. Bloose, who was at that moment triumphantly carrying a pink "shape" into the dining-room which she had been coaxing all the morning to stand up straight in the dish.

Mrs. Bloose was not a prepossessing personage. She would have made a moderately successful monthly nurse. As the Doctor's wife she was a failure. She could not enter into the subtleties of her husband's sermons. To her it mattered little whether Evolution could be made to square with Christianity or Darwin with Moses. But neither could she take a Mother's Meeting nor keep a servant. Thirty-three cooks had come and gone in twenty years, and now she managed the kitchen herself. The Doctor and the dinner suffered in consequence, but as she remarked to the female pew-opener,

"Anything for a quiet life!" In appearance, as some one remarked about her once, she gave one the idea of having been lately dragged through a hedge backwards. Of the joys of this world poor Mrs. Bloose knew little. It was therefore an unusual delight to the good lady, when her husband informed her that Stephen was to be the new curate.

"Fancy a real live lord's son coming to live with us! I must put up the new blue curtains in his lordship's bedroom, and we must have dinner at eight instead of one."

"No, my love," said the Doctor, "we will alter nothing of that kind, because Mr. Remarx is a man of very simple habits, and would like us to go on just as we are. Perhaps, however, Posy and Bob might have their dinners up in the nursery while he is with us, and the tablecloth might be oftener changed. I have noticed that there are a number of mustard stains upon it, and you seem to have forgotten that Bob upset the Harvey's sauce at the north end three weeks ago. Otherwise, my love, let us continue our simple life, even though the Honourable Remarx is coming to stay."

So the "Honourable Remarx" came. There could hardly have been picked out a curacy more contrary to the tastes of Stephen than this of St. Titus, Hoxton. He came up from Oxford brimming over with social enthusiasm. He had studied Political Economy, he had read all the socialistic literature of the day, and devoured his *Daily Chronicle*: he had frequented the Pusey House; he had read both the Booths, the "General" William and the more particular Charles; he had dived into the Reports and attended the meetings in connection with Oxford House and Toynbee Hall; he had formed in his mind an idea of East London Church Work very different from that which he found at St. Titus. He had pictured to himself a crowd of eager students flocking to be taught by Dr. Bloose, atheists, agnostics, secularists, materialists, and theosophists, earnestly argu ing with the Vicar on religious questions, while his wife dealt out soup and bread to a host of the "submerged tenth." He had hoped to find the Doctor well up in all the industrial problems of the hour, consulting with the Union leaders, and offering to arbitrate between employer and employed. He was grievously disappointed. The Doctor, it is true, dealt with the religious difficulties of the day, but only in books and pamphlets which nobody read, or in sermons to which nobody listened. He had never spoken to an East-end atheist in his life. As for educational work, he simply disapproved of it. The Board Schools were to him the especial dwelling-places of Satan, the University Settlements were mistaken attempts to supplant the parochial system; General Booth he considered an impostor, and therefore the "submerged tenth" should be left to starve; while as for the Labour movement, it was a revolution, and ought to be put down by Government.

A few days after his arrival in Hoxton,

Stephen found himself launched into an argument with the Doctor.

"I suppose you often have Tom Mann and Ben Tillett in here, don't you?" said Stephen.

"Who are they?" said Mrs. Bloose innocently.

"My dear," said the Doctor, looking reprovingly at his wife, "go on with your dinner." Then turning to Stephen, he continued, "Mr. Remarx, I am not acquainted with those gentlemen, nor do I want to be; I would as soon admit a convict to my house as them."

"Oh," said Stephen, "I believe they are most agreeable people: besides, there is surely no better way of studying the social question, than to get to know exactly what the leading men on the labour side think and say."

"I have no wish to study the labour side, as you call it, at all," replied the Doctor. "I have studied Adam Smith, Mill, and Ricardo. I am quite convinced that the modern attempts which are being made by the revolutionary party to raise wages artificially, and to drive capital out of the country, must end in terrible disaster and the ruin of England."

"But surely, if you think so, Dr. Bloose," said Stephen, "you ought to do something to ward off this awful calamity, and by way of commencement, would it not be a good thing to make quite sure what it is which the 'revolutionary party,' as you call them, really propose to do? I daresay if you knew some of these bloodthirsty people, you would find them quite harmless and sensible after all."

"Mr. Remarx," said the Doctor, somewhat sternly, "I consider these questions wholly outside a clergyman's sphere of duty. I have other things to do than to be mixing up in all these labour questions."

"But, Doctor, your work as Vicar of St. Titus lies, surely, does it not, almost entirely among working-people, who are intensely interested in these matters? In fact, to them they are questions of bread and butter, of life or slow death, perhaps."

The Doctor looked at his curate with a pitying, patronising gaze. "My dear young man, if you had studied these things in books as I have, and had not simply listened to what ignorant people say, you would know that these men might just as well try to fight against the clock, and attempt to make the time go backwards, as fight against the laws of Political Economy. If they are to starve, starve they will."

"And do you think, then," said Stephen, "that the continuation of our present industrial system is likely to result in the practical starvation of many of the poor?"

"I think it quite likely," said the Doctor, complacently helping himself to a second plate of boiled mutton and capers.

"And yet, as a minister of Christ, who had compassion on the starving multitude, you think it is outside your sphere of duty to attempt even to learn what proposals are being made to prevent this alarming catastrophe."

The Vicar coughed, and Mrs. Bloose, with a tact which she displayed about once in three years, began to talk about the weather. But the good lady's conversational powers were limited, even when devoted to her favourite subject, and at last she ceased.

Stephen very calmly renewed his observations. "It seems to me," he said, "that we, priests and deacons——"

"Priests!" said Mrs. Bloose, interrupting him with a look of dismay, "does the Honourable Remarx refer to the Doctor? Surely, David, you have often told me that there is no priest in the Protestant Church."

"You are right, my dear," said the Doctor, rather glad than otherwise to change the conversation. "Mr. Remarx has doubtless fallen into the error, so common with the younger clergy, of fancying that the word 'priest' in our Book of Common Prayer is a translation of the Latin 'sacerdos.' I, of course, having studied the subject, know that it is a translation of the word 'presbyter,' a very different thing: in fact, the difference is immense."

"Oh, I don't think that will affect what I was going to say," said the Curate. "I will call them presbyters if you prefer it. I was going to say that, in my opinion, we presbyters and deacons should get a thorough knowledge of these social questions, not only from books, but by living contact with the poor themselves" (the Doctor involuntarily shuddered). "In this way we shall be able to help them more effectually."

"Our work," said the Doctor, "is simply and solely to preach the Gospel, and I flatter myself I have done so for twenty years in this place."

"But," said the imperturbable Stephen, "what is the Gospel? Good news, isn't it? Now, what could be better news for these poor people, than to tell them the way out of their troubles?"

"You surely don't mean," said Dr. Bloose, "that you think we ought to get up in the pulpit and preach Socialism? You don't call *that* the Gospel, do you?"

"No," said Stephen, "not exactly that, but I do think it would be more like the Gospel of our Master, if we were to get up in the pulpit and tell them that so far as they want to have proper food and decent homes and opportunities of development, they are only desiring what their heavenly Father wants to give them, and that so far as they are being kept from them, it is because of the selfishness of men who will not do God's will on earth, as it is done in heaven."

"Then do you mean to say," said the Doctor somewhat alarmed, though not a bit convinced, "that you intend to preach discontent to the people?"

"I think," said Stephen, "that there is a Divine discontent that it may be our duty at times to preach, though I confess I would rather preach it in the West than in the East. The rich should be made discontented. God give me the opportunity and courage to do it before I die."

"You have very queer views, young man," said the Vicar, demurely drumming on his plate with the cheese-knife, "very queer views indeed. Where did you pick them up?"

"I have been reading the Prophets and the Gospels," replied Stephen, thoughtfully looking out into the crowded street, "and I have been meditating, that's all."

III

A LECTURE

It must not be supposed that the old Vicar and his young curate were for ever quarrelling, or that any serious feud arose between them. The Doctor was an apostle of *laissez-faire* in parochial as well as in economical matters. He went his way and he let Stephen go his. Occasionally, on a Sunday, he would reprove the young deacon for some of his pulpit utterances, as for example, when he startled the old almspeople by telling them that "to come to Church for what you can get" is an insult to Almighty God, and more likely to land you in hell fire than any amount of honest unbelief," or when he offended the Churchwardens by saying that "the respectable Pharisee, who stalks up the

Church in black cloth and yellow kid gloves and boxes the children's ears while he is singing "Rock of Ages," is a more offensive sight to God's eyes than the poor lost woman in the street."

As a rule, however, Stephen was left to himself to think, and read, and watch and wait. He found out more about the condition of St. Titus' parish in one month, than the Doctor had discovered in twenty years. First of all, he found that it was a hotbed of militant Secularism. While the Vicar was droning away in a black gown on the "Wonders of Creation" to a congregation of twenty on a Sunday morning, Mark Smasham was addressing a crowd of four hundred men in the high road, fifty yards from the Church, on the "Contradictions of Genesis or the Muddles of Moses." While the Biblewoman was flattering herself that her Tuesday evening class of fourteen girls was drawing the young women of Hoxton into the paths of safety, "Mrs. Lucy Grafton, the Peaceful Anarchist," had established an "Institute for Female Citizens, the membership of which had reached two hundred and fifty in a fortnight.

While the Verger's wife had fitted up the disused coal-cellar under the Church as a reading-room for working-men, whither her husband and three of his "pals" resorted to play whist on those nights, when they did not care to go to the "Royal Standard," the "Hoxton Progressives" had opened a Club, where some hundreds of the Doctor's flock might be found any evening of the week enjoying themselves. This sort of thing would have broken the heart of anyone less Christian than Stephen Remarx. To find his beloved Church of England so lamentably in the second place was indeed a trial, but he bore up and manfully went out to fight for his Master. One thought especially buoyed him up. It was this. He knew from personal experience that such a parish as St. Titus was an exception to the general rule. He knew that in other parts of East London the work of social reformation was being led by faithful Church people. He was a personal friend of the workers at the different University Settlements and College Missions. He knew what they were doing, and he knew of the patient, godly labours of many a parish priest. Moreover, he knew that his cause was right. He believed, with an undying conviction, that what these poor men and women wanted was just that which he had to give, and which though at present they seemed not to care for, they would one day feel the need of, the Power of a strong and living Saviour, the Rule of a liberty-loving King. His method of Church work was peculiar. He studied his Prayer-book, and tried to find out what the mind of the Church of England seemed to be. He would argue thus with himself: "The Church does not seem to me so exclusive as I once thought she was; she bids me tell every man, woman and child who has been baptized that they belong to Christ; she seems to picture herself as a great Society, co-extensive almost with the Nation, bound by most strict promises to fight for Christ and right. As I look round this parish, I find very few who appear to be attempting to do this. Of the few who come to Church, only one or two seem to be at all inclined that way. On the other hand, as I look outside at those 'Progressives' and even at the Secularists, I find a number of men who are striving after something very much more like the Truth. They say that they want to make this world a better place, they say they want all men to be treated justly, they say they hate selfishness and admire self-sacrifice, and they practise it too, they say they want each man to be allowed to develop the life that is in him, to think, to read, to know something of the joy of leisure and home and friends, they say that they admire Christ and wish all were like Him. Yes, this was just exactly what the lecturer said at the Club on the night when I went to listen. And they all applauded him, their faces lit up at the thoughts suggested by him. Then they laughed when they saw me, a clergyman, the minister of Christ. But why did they laugh? They did not laugh because they thought I looked like Christ. If they had thought that, they would have applauded me, but they laughed because they thought I was not like Him. They muttered: 'Ah! there's the parson, it's a pity he is not like his Master.'

"I know what I must try and do. I must insert myself into the social life of this place. I must become a member of these Clubs and Institutes. I must go in and out among them. I must try to draw them to believe that they are the Church. I must show them that, so far as their ideals go, they are right and true ones, because they are the ideals of Christ.

"But they must learn to know Him better. And how can they know Him unless I, His minister, can show them what He is? For what else do I exist but to bring men to Christ?"

For three years Stephen lived at Hoxton. During that time, he certainly succeeded in what he called "inserting himself into the social life of the place." He became a well-known character. The old church was full when it was rumoured that "the curate" was going to preach, and the Doctor gradually left off attempting to compete with him. An accommodating physician was found, who discovered that "three weeks at Brighton" were periodically necessary for the life of the Vicar. They were certainly conducive to the life of the parish, for they meant "Mr. Remarx in sole charge," and that meant a full church and an eager congregation. Then, too, he would go out Sunday after Sunday into the high road and preach after Mark Smasham had finished his orations. It was noticed by many that Mark's meeting was not so well attended as in old days. "We like to hear Mr. Stephen," the men would say, " he's got something to tell us." Frequently, too, the young curate would mount the platform at the "Progressive Club," but he never spoke on a social subject without reminding them of Christ. Thus they got to feel that 'there was a real difference between his lectures, and those which they were accustomed to hear from others. Stephen's gave his hearers the impression that, at any rate in his opinion, something more was wanted than material improvement for the masses.

So genuine was the impression which Stephen was making on the life and thought of the place, that it became necessary for the Secularists to take steps to counteract his influence. A leading lecturer was engaged to speak at the "Institute for Female Citizens," opened "for this occasion only" to reformers of both sexes. As the lecture had a great effect on the mind of Stephen himself, more perhaps than it had on the minds of the remainder of the audience, it has been thought well to give some extracts from it.

The subject of the lecture was announced thus: "*Why we cannot become Christians.*" The lecturer began with a vigorous description of the aims and objects of social reformers. "There is,' he said, "a social question; no one except

A LECTURE

a fool can altogether shut his eyes to what is going on around him. We have certain ghastly facts staring us in the face. There is the ghastly fact of a few men rolling in riches, and absolutely not knowing what to do with their wealth, side by side with a multitude of others so poor that they cannot live a decent life. I am not only alluding to the so-called 'submerged' portion of the community, but I speak of the crowds of men and women with good characters and abilities who are willing to do but unable to get work. We are surrounded in this East-end of ours by people who are slowly dying from insufficient food, who are denied the barest necessities of existence, whose lives are one perpetual yearning after work which seldom comes, who have got no hearts left for pleasure, or study, or any of the possible joys of humanity. I speak of the men and women, the young lads and girls, who, if they have got work, must be content to accept it in such a form that it is scarcely distinguishable from slavery. Ladies and gentlemen," continued the lecturer, "none but the careless 'masher,' whose tailor's bill will always be paid by his father if he runs through his allowance, the popular professional lawyer who will never want a brief, the fashionable doctor whose patients are legion, and his fee two guineas, the retired money-grubber, the hereditary millionaire, none but such as these can dare to shut their eyes and say that there is no social question. I need not waste my time in proving it. Even the Bishop believe it." (This he said with a twinkle in his eye and the audience laughed.)

"Now comes the question: 'Is there no remedy?' Well, I am not an extreme man, I am not an optimist, I do not think we shall make things better all in a day but I do think we can find out the line on which we ought to work, I do think that our children's children may enjoy a happier life than we do.

"We believe that Parliament can do much for us. There are some of our laws which want changing. We want more laws for the benefit of the worker. The capitalist and the landlord have had it all their own way too long. Yes, the Democracy will look after itself. Education will teach us what we have a right to, Science is showing us what we are, and what we are meant to be. We are willing to be helped in our social endeavours by all those who will work for the common good. And this brings me to the subject of my lecture—'Why we cannot be Christians.'

"I understand that lately, in this neighbourhood, there has been an attempt made by a minister of the Established religion to persuade people that the true panacea for all our social evils is Christianity. I will at once say that, so far as this reverend gentleman will help us to solve the social problem, I am glad to welcome him as a brother, but as regards his panacea, I must say I do not believe in it.

"I have come here to-night to give you my reasons for not believing in Christianity as a social reforming agency at the present juncture. Mark you, I do not intend to-night to question the fact that Christianity has had a certain effect upon the world, though I am prepared to maintain that civilisation has done much more. I do not deny that there was once a remarkable man called Christ, who said some startling things to which nobody pays any attention now. But I do not believe that we should be any nearer the solution of the social problem if we became Christians. These are my reasons. First, we are in the great difficulty of not exactly knowing what Christianity is. Is it the Christianity of Christ which is to reform the world, or is it the Christianity of the Middle Ages which is to do it? Or is it the Christianity of Mr. Spurgeon, or of Mr. Moody, or of Dr. Pusey, or of Dr. Bloose? Or has this new teacher who has come to live here lately got a new form of Christianity which he alone knows all about? Supposing we all follow him and become Christians, according to his gospel, how are we to know that the Bishop of London will not come down upon us and say, 'That's not Christianity at all; you have got hold of the wrong thing altogether.'

"But granting that the Christianity which we are asked to accept is the Christianity of Christ pure and simple, I immediately proceed to ask my friend to show us how it's done. I look in vain for the example of a Christ-like Christian. We people down here in East London are looked upon as unchristian, so I will not expect to find what I want here. But I will look at some of these West-end Churches or these Universities, who profess to have got hold of something which they are kind enough to wish to send us down here. If this is not so, why do they establish these Missions and settlements at considerable cost to themselves? But where are the poverty and simplicity, where is the hatred of sham and hypocrisy, where is the love of the outcast, which ought surely to be found in the followers of the Carpenter of Nazareth?

"I challenge my friend to show me a

single man or woman among the fashionable Church congregations in the West-end, or in the academic circles at Oxford and Cambridge (whence these Missions come), a single man or woman, I say, who is living a life at all like Christ's, or who is even attempting to carry out certain of the commands of their Master which I shall be ready to enumerate if required. Where is there a man, for instance, who has given up all that he possesses for the sake of Christianity? Where is there a man who has forsaken father and mother and lands for the sake of what Christ calls the Kingdom of Heaven? No, my friends, we cannot be Christians!

"But perhaps my opponent would answer, as in fact I did hear a Bishop say the other day: 'You have no right to argue against Christianity from the failure of Christians. You must show that Christianity itself is a failure.'

"Very well, I am prepared to maintain that too. First, my friends, consider what it is that Christianity claims to be

A LECTURE

able to do. These Christian Socialists tell us that our plans for social reform will fail because we take no account of the moral reformation which is necessary before any change of circumstances will avail. In a word, we must wait till a man is good before we make him comfortable. Personally, I think it would be better to reverse the process. Let us make him comfortable, give him a decent home, leisure and a moderate wage, and then perhaps he will be good. However, let us examine the Christian argument. They say in effect, 'Give the people to us, we will make them good: if they are not good, all your social reforms will fail.' Well, now, before we hand over the people to the tender care of Mother Church, my friends, I want to have some guarantee that she is likely to succeed in what she claims to be able to do. I look back into past history, and I do not find that the world progressed more satisfactorily when the Church held full sway over it. I look into recent social history, do I find that reforms have been initiated by the Church? Not a bit of it. More often than not the Church has opposed them. What social reforms have my lords, the Bishops, ever proposed? I might add, 'What have they not opposed?' It is true that individual Christians, like Lord Shaftesbury, have done good social work, but he was not the Church.

"The fact is, my friends, that Christianity has had its chance and has missed the mark. We gave it free play once, and it came off blank. Some of us got burnt in the process by this social reforming agency. Are we so very unreasonable if we turn round now and say, 'Never again, my friends; you have had your opportunity and you have shown that your system is a fraud and a delusion. Henceforth, we turn to other helpers: The State, the Voice of the People, the discoveries of Science. These are our guiding lights. We do not need you!' Don't be taken in, ladies and gentlemen, by the specious proposals of these so-called Christian

A LECTURE

Socialists who talk about Christ, the poor working-man, who had not where to lay his head, while they themselves, who claim to represent Him, have never been without a comfortable bed in their lives. Let them show us what He was like, and then, perhaps, we may listen; but even then the Christianity which they propose for us must be something very different from the Christianity of the past, if it is to solve the problem."

"He's very wrong and very right," thought Stephen, as he walked back to the Vicarage. "What if, after all, our Missions are wrongly directed? Ought we to go to the West-end? But surely our Lord would have us preach to the poor? Yes, but how can we preach Him until we know Him better? 'Can the blind lead the blind; shall they not both fall into the ditch?'"

IV

WESTWARD HO!

THE Marquis of St. Alphege possessed no charms of his own. He was ugly, sour, and foul-mouthed. He was a Tory of the old school, and had an apoplectic fit on hearing that a Conservative Government had granted Free Education to the masses. He recovered from the fit, but he would never read the newspaper again, nor go to the House of Lords. His language had always been unparliamentary, his whole life thenceforth became so. The nation, it must be confessed, seemed to have lost little, when this hereditary law-maker ceased to impress the red leather cushions of the Upper House. His lordship had however, other possessions, to wit, a handsome wife, thirty years younger than himself, and a magnificent mansion in Chelsea Square. The Marchioness was a leader in Society; but, mark you, not *of* Society. She had a set of her own choosing, and only these ever passed within the portals of Alphege House.

They were an interesting set: there was a Broad Church Dean, a High Church Canon, the Secretary of an unsectarian Orphanage, and the Actor-Manager of the Grand Theatre; while for ladies, there were the Lady Warden of the Ladies' Settlement in Wapping, the Secretary of the Ladies' League, the Duchess of Lundy and Dr. Frances Deane. Besides these more prominent ones, there were lesser lights, most of them men and women with fads. Her ladyship dearly loved a fad. She would spend hours of an afternoon on her sofa, listening to the latest ideas of the latest faddist, and remarking at intervals: "Dear me, how intensely interesting. I must introduce you to the Dean; he will be so charmed with your idea."

Quite wrongly, though somewhat excusably, the Marchioness reckoned her nephew Stephen among this curious army of fad-mongers. "You ought to know my nephew, Mr. Remarx, he is quite supernaturally clever, he has such original ideas; though I must confess he wears the most sacrilegious trousers; I wish he would go to Alfy's tailor in Conduit Street."

In spite of his dress, the Marchioness really loved her nephew with all the affection that a shallow nature can bestow. She saw, with the instinct of a fashionable leader, that he was likely to cause a sensation, if cautiously introduced into London society. Her opportunity came when the important living of St. Mark and the Angels fell vacant by the death of Dr. Oldskin. The benefice was in the gift of the Marquis of St. Alphege, the parish being, in fact, almost co-extensive with his property in Chelsea.

"Alfy, dear," said the Marchioness to her lord at breakfast, "when you have finished your kidneys, will you listen to me?"

"Go on," said the venerable peer.

"Have you thought of any one for St. Mark's yet, Alfy?" Her ladyship knew how to manage him. It was her way to make him think he was the master and not she.

"Yes," said the Marquis, handling a pile of letters. "I have here applications from two hundred and twenty parsons for the place; everybody seems to want it. One blackguard is certainly more candid than the rest. He says he can't pay his bills, and his wife's a confirmed invalid, and his eldest boy's in debt, and will I help him out of his financial difficulties by making him Vicar of St. Mark's. Upon my honour, I've a good mind to give it him, if only because of such a straightforward declaration of his object. There's another one here I like, who says he's a thorough-going Tory, and thinks the Primrose League much too democratic, and that he has proved beyond question that Babylon in the Apocalypse is a prophecy of the London County Council." The Marquis gobbled a piece of *pâté de foie gras* on toast and stopped. Then the Marchioness began to play her cards.

"Have you thought of Stephen, in connection with the post?"

"No, I can't say I have," said his lordship, "but he's very well provided for, isn't he? I never bother myself about him."

Then out came her ladyship's trumps. She represented that for the honour of the family Stephen ought to be a rector, that it was absurd for an "Honourable" to be a curate in the slums; that the reports about his being High Church were not well founded; that he quite believed in the Lincoln Judgment; that there was no real proof that he was a Radical or a Socialist. The Marchioness very nearly choked when she said this, for it was only three days before, that Stephen had actually advised her to read the "Fabian Essays," and had described to her how he had taken the chair at a "Progressive" meeting in Clerkenwell.

"Well, hang it," said the Marquis with a levity scarcely consistent with the sacred duty of appointing a spiritual father for twelve thousand souls, " hang it, I don't care who has the beastly living: all parsons are equally cussed in my eyes, nowadays." The rest of the sentence contained so many bad words that it has been thought better not to reproduce it.

"May I write and ask Stephen?" said the Marchioness.

"You may do anything you confounded like." This elegant phrase decided the spiritual prospects of the twelve thousand parishioners, and the triumphant peeress retired to her boudoir to pen the following letter, remarkable alike for its grammar and gush:

"My very dear Ste.

"I have a very delicious pleasure in having to write and tell you, that the old 'Markis' offers you the living of St. Mark's. Of course you will take it. It is very much better than where you are.

It is worth £800 a year, and there is a good rectory. Of course, Oldskin's furniture is bad, and his taste was execrable, but Maples will make that all right. I should have a light blue damask paper in the drawing-room, and get rid of that spotted linoleum on the staircase. You must have four curates. I think the Bishop has some fund that will pay for them. They will do what I call the drudgery of the work. You must of course keep yourself for preaching on Sunday. Fancy how splendid to have you taking the town by storm. I would have a short service at half-past eleven, if I were you, just an anthem or something, and then a spicy sermon full of all sorts of good advice about our weaknesses; the dear Duchess of Lundy is so fond of that sort of thing, don't you know, and so am I for the matter of that, and then we could get into the Park by a quarter to one, and get the luncheon party well begun before two, which I always think is so important. I must not go on like this or I shall tire you. Now, mind you say yes. If you like to come and see me, I have got Chevallier la Trobe to tea at 4.30 to-morrow. He has got a new idea about having a psychological Congress. Do come and we can talk about St. Mark's. By-the-bye I believe the drains want looking at.

"Yours most affectionately,

"AUNT ALF.

"P.S.—I think the pews bring in another £200, but I'm not sure."

Thus it was that Stephen became the Rector of St. Mark's.

V

THE DOCKER

It was the "Sing song" night at the Wapping "Tee-to-tum." A "Tee-to-tum" may be shortly described as a Working Men's Club without alcohol, a Restaurant without bad coffee, and a Tea Shop without tea dust. You can generally depend upon getting your money's worth if you go to a "Tee-to-tum," though the music that night was not of a very high class character. The performers, it is true, belonged to the very highest classes: there was more than one titled lady and gentleman among them, but somehow they had concocted a curious programme. The banjo songs were not exactly bad, but neither were they refined, the skirt-dancing by Lady Blanche

Breezer was, to say the least of it, rather queer, while the comic songs condescendingly read by the Hon. Arthur Jones were, strange to say, the very same, which "Geoffrey Crump the Inimitable" had sung at the "Paragon" the night before, at least so the boys at the back of the hall said. Now, if you had gone to the Wellington Club that night at 12 o'clock, and asked these ladies and gentlemen, as they sat at supper discussing champagne and oysters, how they had occupied the earlier part of the evening, they would have told you no doubt that they had been "elevating the masses!" Poor dears! and yet they meant well. "It's so good for the people to come in contact with our class," the Duchess of Lundy had said to Lady Blanche: "do try and get up a Concert for them down at Wapping, you can manage it easily after Ascot is over, only take care, my dear, that you put on an old gown, you might catch something." Thus the Concert came off. And it produced one important result. It led two men to converse with, and to get to know one another, who before had been but slightly acquainted. These were Paul Durnford and John Oxenham. They sat in the concert-room, and submitted themselves to the process known as "elevation."

Paul Durnford had been one of Stephen's companions at Oxford. His father was a carpenter in Dorsetshire, and Paul had worked his way up by sheer hard labour. He had won numberless Scholarships, and had earned enough to keep him at Oxford until he took a First Class in Modern History. At the period of the Wapping concert, he was staying in East London at one of the University Settlements, in order to become acquainted with "the people." He had had the good fortune to be appointed head librarian to a new public library, then being built in one of the East-End parishes, and he was in the happy position of having the prospect of plenty of useful work to do, and a sufficient income.

His neighbour in the concert-room was a dock labourer. John Oxenham had been one of the leaders in the great Dock strike, and had the reputation of being very "advanced" in his views. It was quite by chance that he had strolled into the "Tee-to-tum" that night, and taken his seat by the side of Paul.

"This sort of thing won't solve the social problem, will it?" said Oxenham bluntly to his neighbour. They had met before, at the time of the strike, when Paul was occupied in giving out grocery tickets to the dockers' wives.

"No, I don't think it will," said Paul, as Lady Blanche entered upon the last verse of "Ta-ra-ra-boom-de-ay."

"What fools the men are," said Oxenham, "to believe in these aristocrats: it's all chloroform, that's what it is."

"Chloroform, what do you mean by that?" inquired Durnford.

"Why, I mean just this," said the other, "these nobs are in a mortal funk of us workers. That there Lady Blanche and her Jezebel of a mother, the Duchess, are Dames of the Primrose League: now, they think if they can keep us quiet by giving us concerts and tea-meetings, we shall be induced to rest content and say nothing, while they are up to their larks in the West-end. It's chloroform to keep us asleep, that's what it is. But it's too late," said the Strike leader half starting to his feet, with his eyes gleaming, as if he would like to storm the platform; "it's too late, they ought to have thought of it long ago, if they wanted it to succeed, they ought to have thought of it before the Education Act, and before we got the vote: we don't want their soup tickets. I hate these West-end Missionaries and Settlements. Settlements indeed! the very word suggests that we are savages."

"Knocked 'em in the Old Kent Road," screamed Lady Blanche, with a bewitching curl of her blue-blooded lip, and sat down amid roars of applause.

"I can't stand it," said Oxenham, "come outside, Mr. Durnford, and let's have a walk, the very air here chokes me."

They walked down the street together in silence. "Don't you think," said Paul at last, "that you are a little hard on us?"

"Hard on *you?*" said Oxenham, with a look of disgust, "why, you surely don't class yourself with that gang, do you?"

"Well, no, not exactly," said Paul, "but still I am an Oxford man, and I am one of those who, in a humble way, are trying to contribute something towards the solution of the social problem, and I belong, you know, to one of those 'Settlements' about which you talked so disparagingly just now."

Oxenham looked at Paul, and said quite calmly, and with an earnestness, that his companion had not noticed in his former utterances, "Mr. Durnford, you're as different from that painted step-dancer, as that full moon yonder is from a dinner-plate."

Paul said nothing. His companion went on: "I have been face to face with the social problem now, for many years.

I have felt the injustice of our social system as much as any man alive. I have seen both sides, for I used to live on the estate of a rich lord. My father was his gardener. I did odd jobs in the house, and I know how the aristocracy live. Their feeding arrangements, alone, would drive me into socialism. Four square meals a day, if you please, for my lord's family, while the poor dockers, out of whose labour my lord gets his screw, for you must know he's a large shareholder, both in docks and ships, the poor dockers, I say, are literally starving. My lord seldom spoke of the dockers, except to call them a 'drunken, lazy lot.' Mr. Durnford, I have seen my lord's own sons the worse for liquor, I have seen them play cards for money until 4 A.M., I have known them lie in bed till noon, I have never known them to do an hour's useful work for the good of mankind in their lives."

"May I speak?" said Paul, for he felt that his companion was having it too much his own way: "I too can speak from experience: I too am a poor man the son of a carpenter."

"I respect you for that," said Oxenham, taking off his hat quite seriously, and not in play.

Paul continued: "I have seen many good and kind rich people. Is it not better in discussing social problems to keep from personalities, and to stick to principles? There are good and bad people on both sides. There are drunken dockers, but there are respectable ones too, as I can vouch for, just as there are drunken and dissolute sons of peers, and some very good ones also. The attack must be made on the system, not on the persons who are the victims of it."

"You are right, Mr. Durnford, but my blood was up; you see it was those young lordlings that I knew in my youth, who first started me on the socialistic war path, and I can't forget them."

"Well, forget them now," said Paul, "and let's talk deeper. Don't you think that sympathy between classes is the very first thing to be established before any of this brushwood of injustice and inequality can be cleared away? Now, it is just this sympathy which these settlements and these social gatherings have done so much to foster. Lady Blanche Breezer may have rather a vulgar, boisterous way of showing her sympathy, but I daresay she has a good heart."

"Don't talk to me of that woman," growled John, "we'll leave her out if you please; you said just now we were to keep from personalities, and her ladyship's personality is just what I can't abide. Now, I daresay I may have been wrong about the settlements. If all these philanthropists were like yourself, I should not mind. Yours is a genuine sympathy, because you are a poor man yourself. Nobody can sympathise unless he has really experienced the sufferings of those whom he proposes to compassionate. I, for instance, have often been hungry myself, and that's why I could lead the strike."

"Oxenham," said Durnford seriously, "in that last sentence of yours you have touched upon what I believe to be the very key of the social problem."

"What do you mean?" said John.

"I mean that when you talk of the necessity of sympathy, you suggest to me the thought of Christianity, the religion which centres round One whose very life was sympathy itself."

"Are you a Christian?" asked the docker. "I mean, a real Christian—not one of these sham ones who cover the face of the earth."

"I am trying to be," said Paul, in a simple, unaffected way.

"But does your religion," said Oxenham, "help you at all in your social aspirations? It always seems to me such an unpractical affair; the clergy are always talking about Heaven above and all that sort of thing. I call them sky pilots."

"Do you know Mr. Remarx?" said Paul abruptly.

"No," said John.

"I wish you did," said Durnford, "I will take you next Sunday to hear him preach."

VI

IN THE WILDERNESS

STEPHEN certainly created a sensation, though hardly in the way the Marchioness had contemplated. There were several strict rules he made for himself, which did not at all suit his aunt's ideas of what a popular preacher ought to do and to be. He absolutely refused ever to come to her Sunday luncheon parties. This she consoled herself about by saying to the Duchess: "Well, my dear, at any rate we shall be able to talk about the sermon better in my nephew's absence!" But then he so often could not come even to dinner or tea. In the afternoons he wanted to visit the poor, and in the evenings he would insist on looking after his gymnasium. "My dear Ste," Aunt

Alfy would say, "you'll simply kill yourself. Dr. Oldskin never did that kind of work, and he came of quite a low family. I believe his mother was a laundress. Now, if *he* did not work, why need you?" Stephen would then gently remind her that there were no less than eight thousand poor people in St. Mark's parish, or he would read her portions of the Ordination Service to impress upon her his responsibilities. Then she would try another tack. "My dear, you must remember that you have a duty towards the rich members of your parish, you seem to forget them. I always say, we rich people want quite as much looking after as the lower classes." "And a great deal more, sometimes!" thought Stephen, but he would answer her thus aloud," Aunt Alfy, I don't think you quite understand the nature of a clergyman's work. I have but one object, namely, to preach and to teach Christ. Now, my method of doing this with poor and rich may differ a little according to circumstances. In the first place, I find them in very different attitudes towards Christianity by reason of their opportunities. Most of my rich parishioners have had the Gospel preached to them, and have learnt their Catechism, while most of my poor people have hardly heard it at all, or are deeply prejudiced against the Church itself. And so it comes, that with one set of persons my work is to break down prejudice or to attract them into Church, while with the other, it is to get them to carry out in practice the religion they already know about, but whose principles they have no desire to apply to life."

"I don't understand," said the Marchioness, vacantly.

"Let me then give you a few examples. Take such a man as Sir Henry Dyvese. He is the Chairman of the 'National Security Match Company.' He is a nominal Christian, who gives at least eighteenpence to the collection on Sunday, and believes in the great importance of an Established Church. It is true he never kneels down, but he says very fervently, after each of the ten commandments, 'Incline our hearts to keep this law.' But for all this, he won't move a finger to remedy the grievances of the girls he employs. Four of these girls last week were suffering from a sore mouth, which comes from making matches in a way that might be avoided. Their wages, too, would hardly pay for the keep of Lady Dyvese's collie; and yet the ordinary shareholders are receiving 15 per cent."

"I really do not see what this has to do with religion," said her ladyship, almost pettishly.

"Wait a minute," said Stephen. "My duty is somehow or other to bring it home to Sir Henry, that his religion requires him to look into these matters, and that he might just as well be a Mohammedan, if he does not. In fact, I said as much to him the other day."

"What did he say?" asked the Aunt.

"He laughed, and said that the clergy

were notoriously bad men of business, and had better not interfere where they were not wanted."

"A very good answer," laughed the Marchioness.

"It satisfied him," said Stephen sternly, "but it did not satisfy me. However, let's take another case—a more general one. All you ladies are very particular about having your dresses made to time; sometimes you give the poor dressmaker very little time in which to execute your orders, or you haggle over the price of things, and clutch at what is cheap. Now, does it never strike you that you are really responsible for the excessively long hours during which some poor people have to slave, and for the low wages they are paid, and for the bad conditions under which some of them have to work? Do you know, for instance, that at Smith and Jobley's shop, where, I believe, you get many of your things, the shop-girls are never allowed to sit down, and that they work ninety hours a week? Only last night, I was at the death-bed of a poor girl who used to work there. She is dying of consumption, brought on simply by her hard work."

"Oh, well, of course I think that's all very dreadful," said the poor Marchioness, who was beginning to feel quite uncomfortable, "but I cannot do anything; Alfy says that political economy teaches us that we must let things go on, and that you cannot fight against what he calls the 'iron laws.' I don't know what he means, but dear Ste, do take some port wine to that poor girl."

"She has all she wants in that way," said Stephen seriously, and then looking earnestly at his worldly aunt, he went on: "Aunt Alfy, I know you have a good kind heart; I know you want to help those poor people, but I am convinced that something more is wanted than the giving of material aid. We must change our lives, we must give ourselves for them, and not only our money to them; we must, in fact, live as Christ-lived, yes, even here in this nineteenth-century London. Dear

Aunt, will you help me? Will you try with me?" He said this in a tremulous, hesitating voice, only too conscious that such an appeal would be quite lost on his fashionable relation.

"My dear boy, I can make no promises."

Fortunately, at this moment the luncheon-bell rang and the Marchioness went to wash her hands.

"I can make no promises!" mused Stephen. "But she has made them already, and so have I. We promised at our baptism to renounce the world, the flesh, and the devil. What are we doing to keep them?"

It may seem surprising that Stephen should have spoken thus seriously to his aunt. One might have thought that he would have looked for more earnest spirits, before whom to cast his pearls. The truth was that Stephen had made few friends. He was living a solitary life. Crowds, it is true, came to his church, but at present they just came and went away. They discussed his sermons in private; some tried to pick to pieces his startling theories, some pondered over them alone. Old-fashioned Church people began by having uneasy thoughts that perhaps he might be right, but they generally ended by settling satisfactorily to their own consciences that his eccentric doctrines were the outcome of what they called his "hot-headed youth." The younger people, especially the young men who came in considerable numbers on Sunday mornings, were more deeply impressed by what he said. Some of them who had been sceptically inclined at first would say: "Well, if Christianity is what Remarx says it is, there is much more in it than ever I dreamt of." This attractive power of Stephen was not because he compromised his faith or made his message palatable to his hearers. No one was more orthodox or unswerving in his allegiance to the grand supernatural truths of the Christian Creed. Rather it was because he made the Creed a living thing, entering into all the details of every-day human life, showing single man or woman among the fashionable Church congregations in the Westend, or in the academic circles at Oxford and Cambridge (whence these Missions come), a single man or woman, I say, who is living a life at all like Christ's, or who is even attempting to carry out certain of the commands of their Master which I shall be ready to enumerate if required. Where is there a man, for instance, who has given up all that he possesses for the sake of Christianity? Where is there a man who has forsaken father and mother and lands for the sake of what Christ calls the Kingdom of Heaven? No, my friends, we cannot be Christians!

"But perhaps my opponent would answer, as in fact I did hear a Bishop say the other day: 'You have no right to argue against Christianity from the failure of Christians. You must show that Christianity itself is a failure.'

"Very well, I am prepared to maintain that too. First, my friends, consider what it is that Christianity claims to be able to do. These Christian Socialists tell us that our plans for social reform will fail because we take no account of the moral reformation which is necessary before any change of circumstances will avail. In a word, we must wait till a man is good before we make him comfortable. Personally, I think it would be better to reverse the process. Let us make him comfortable, give him a decent home, leisure and a moderate wage, and then perhaps he will be good. However, let us examine the Christian argument. They say in effect, 'Give the people to us, we will make them good: if they are not good, all your social reforms will fail.' Well, now, before we hand over the people to the tender care of Mother Church, my friends, I want to have some guarantee that she is likely to succeed in what she claims to be able to do. I look back into past history, and I do not find that the world progressed more satisfactorily when the Church held full sway over it. I look into recent social history, do I find that reforms have been initiated by the Church? Not a bit of it. More often than not the Church has opposed them. What social reforms have my lords, the Bishops, ever proposed? I might add, 'What have they not opposed?' It is true that individual Christians, like Lord Shaftesbury, have done good social work, but he was not the Church.

"The fact is, my friends, that Christianity has had its chance and has missed the mark. We gave it free play once, and it came off blank. Some of us got burnt in the process by this social reforming agency. Are we so very unreasonable if we turn round now and say, 'Never again, my friends; you have had your opportunity and you have shown that your system is a fraud and a delusion. Henceforth, we turn to other helpers: The State, the Voice of the People, the discoveries of Science. These are our guiding lights. We do not need you!' Don't be taken in, ladies and gentlemen, by the specious proposals of these so-called Christian

A LECTURE

Socialists who talk about Christ, the poor working-man, who had not where to lay his head, while they themselves, who claim to represent Him, have never been without a comfortable bed in their lives. Let them show us what He was like, and then, perhaps, we may listen; but even then the Christianity which they propose for us must be something very different from the Christianity of the past, if it is to solve the problem."

"He's very wrong and very right," thought Stephen, as he walked back to the Vicarage. "What if, after all, our Missions are wrongly directed? Ought we to go to the West-end? But surely our Lord would have us preach to the poor? Yes, but how can we preach Him until we know Him better? 'Can 'the blind lead the blind; shall they not both fall into the ditch?'"

IV

WESTWARD HO!

THE Marquis of St. Alphege possessed no charms of his own. He was ugly, sour, and foul-mouthed. He was a Tory of the old school, and had an apoplectic fit on hearing that a Conservative Government had granted Free Education to the masses. He recovered from the fit, but he would never read the newspaper again, nor go to the House of Lords. His language had always been unparliamentary, his whole life thenceforth became so. The nation, it must be confessed, seemed to have lost little, when this hereditary law-maker ceased to impress the red leather cushions of the Upper House. His lordship had however, other possessions, to wit, a handsome wife, thirty years younger than himself, and a magnificent mansion in Chelsea Square. The Marchioness was a leader in Society; but, mark you, not *of* Society. She had a set of her own choosing, and only these ever passed within the portals of Alphege House.

They were an interesting set : there was a Broad Church Dean, a High Church Canon, the Secretary of an unsectarian Orphanage, and the Actor-Manager of the Grand Theatre; while for ladies, there were the Lady Warden of the Ladies' Settlement in Wapping, the Secretary of the Ladies' League, the Duchess of Lundy and Dr. Frances Deane. Besides these more prominent ones, there were lesser lights, most of them men and women with fads. Her ladyship dearly loved a fad. She would spend hours of an afternoon on her sofa, listening to the latest ideas of the latest faddist, and remarking at intervals: "Dear me, how intensely interesting. I must introduce you to the Dean; he will be so charmed with your idea."

Quite wrongly, though somewhat excusably, the Marchioness reckoned her nephew Stephen among this curious army of fad-mongers. "You ought to know my nephew, Mr. Remarx, he is quite supernaturally clever, he has such original ideas; though I must confess he wears the most sacrilegious trousers; I wish he would go to Alfy's tailor in Conduit Street."

In spite of his dress, the Marchioness really loved her nephew with all the affection that a shallow nature can bestow. She saw, with the instinct of a fashionable leader, that he was likely to cause a sensation, if cautiously introduced into London society. Her opportunity came when the important living of St. Mark and the Angels fell vacant by the death of Dr. Oldskin. The benefice was in the gift of the Marquis of St. Alphege, the parish being, in fact, almost co-extensive with his property in Chelsea.

"Alfy, dear," said the Marchioness to her lord at breakfast, "when you have finished your kidneys, will you listen to me?"

"Go on," said the venerable peer.

"Have you thought of any one for St. Mark's yet, Alfy?" Her ladyship knew how to manage him. It was her way to make him think he was the master and not she.

"Yes," said the Marquis, handling a pile of letters. "I have here applications from two hundred and twenty parsons for the place; everybody seems to want it. One blackguard is certainly more candid than the rest. He says he can't pay his bills, and his wife's a confirmed invalid, and his eldest boy's in debt, and will I help him out of his financial difficulties by making him Vicar of St. Mark's. Upon my honour, I've a good mind to give it him, if only because of such a straightforward declaration of his object. There's another one here I like, who says he's a thorough-going Tory, and thinks the Primrose League much too democratic, and that he has proved beyond question that Babylon in the Apocalypse is a prophecy of the London County Council." The Marquis gobbled a piece of *pâté de foie gras* on toast and stopped. Then the Marchioness began to play her cards.

"Have you thought of Stephen, in connection with the post?"

"No, I can't say I have," said his lordship, "but he's very well provided for, isn't he? I never bother myself about him."

Then out came her ladyship's trumps. She represented that for the honour of the family Stephen ought to be a rector, that it was absurd for an "Honourable" to be a curate in the slums; that the reports about his being High Church were not well founded; that he quite believed in the Lincoln Judgment; that there was no real proof that he was a Radical or a Socialist. The Marchioness very nearly choked when she said this, for it was only three days before, that Stephen had actually advised her to read the "Fabian Essays," and had described to her how he had taken the chair at a "Progressive" meeting in Clerkenwell.

"Well, hang it," said the Marquis with a levity scarcely consistent with the sacred duty of appointing a spiritual father for twelve thousand souls, "hang it, I don't care who has the beastly living: all parsons are equally cussed in my eyes, nowadays." The rest of the sentence contained so many bad words that it has been thought better not to reproduce it.

"May I write and ask Stephen?" said the Marchioness.

"You may do anything you confounded like." This elegant phrase decided the spiritual prospects of the twelve thousand parishioners, and the triumphant peeress retired to her boudoir to pen the following letter, remarkable alike for its grammar and gush:

"MY VERY DEAR STE.

"I have a very delicious pleasure in having to write and tell you, that the old 'Markis' offers you the living of St. Mark's. Of course you will take it. It is very much better than where you are.

It is worth £800 a year, and there is a good rectory. Of course, Oldskin's furniture is bad, and his taste was execrable, but Maples will make that all right. I should have a light blue damask paper in the drawing-room, and get rid of that spotted linoleum on the staircase. You must have four curates. I think the Bishop has some fund that will pay for them. They will do what I call the drudgery of the work. You must of course keep yourself for preaching on Sunday. Fancy how splendid to have you taking the town by storm. I would have a short service at half-past eleven, if I were you, just an anthem or something, and then a spicy sermon full of all sorts of good advice about our weaknesses; the dear Duchess of Lundy is so fond of that sort of thing, don't you know, and so am I for the matter of that, and then we could get into the Park by a quarter to one, and get the luncheon party well begun before two, which I always think is so important. I must not go on like this or I shall tire you. Now, mind you say yes. If you like to come and see me, I have got Chevallier la Trobe to tea at 4.30 to-morrow. He has got a new idea about having a psychological Congress. Do come and we can talk about St. Mark's. By-the-bye I believe the drains want looking at.

"Yours most affectionately,
"AUNT ALF.

"P.S.—I think the pews bring in another £200, but I'm not sure."

Thus it was that Stephen became the Rector of St. Mark's.

world any one that looks like Christ, or anything that looks like what we read of in the Gospels. I think if people could only feel that we were really doing what our Lord did they would believe in us. The modern philanthropist never seems to me to have one point in common with his Master. He is not even hated and he will never be crucified. I cannot express it exactly, but perhaps you can guess what I mean."

Stephen was profoundly agitated. He could scarcely control himself. "Oxenham," he almost shouted, "I know it, I know it: you have guessed my meaning: it is what I long for, what I pray for. To show Christ to the world. When men look at me, they see a clergyman; perhaps to them that means nothing more than a State-paid preacher, who does not even believe what he is paid to say; but what ought they to see? They should see Christ. They should see a man full of compassion and long suffering, a man honestly indignant at hypocrisy and sham, hating evil, wholly devoted to righteousness, a man stripped of earthly wealth and comfort, a poor man yet making many rich. Ah yes, and everywhere in this Christian Church there should be Christs, men and women, boys and girls, separate from this devilish world spirit, employers of labour with clean hands and pure hearts, statesmen honest and single-hearted, women pure and kind, artists and labourers diligent and truthful, every one loving, every one working. Great God, can it be done? Who will help me? who will help me?" He sank on the sofa and shed great brave tears of manly strength.

"I will help you," said Oxenham calmly, "through Christ our Lord."

VIII

IN EXCELSIS

THE coverts at Lundy Towers had got to be shot for the second time of the season. This important truth had impressed itself on the mind of the Duchess a month ago, and Her Grace had been busily engaged, for two hours every day between late breakfast and early lunch, in scheming and planning for this great event. "First, the shooting men must be asked: Captain Deadly from the Depot, Lord Henry and Lord Arthur from the Abbey, and that horrid Radical Vesey Maitland, whom the Duke always insists on having, because he's such a good shot. These and the two boys will be enough for the coverts." So argued the Duchess with herself. "Then there's the House party. I must have the Marchioness, and I am afraid Mary will be offended if I don't ask her and her two hideous girls. What a trouble relations are, to be sure!"

"They are so horribly good too, those Bramley girls," said Lady Blanche; "they'll be giving away tracts in the drawing-room after dinner as sure as I'm a Breezer."

"My dear Blanche," said her Grace, "as if I should allow such a thing! Still, of course, their religion is most objectionable, so very different from the sensible doctrines of our Prayer Book."

If her Grace had been narrowly questioned as to what those "sensible doctrines" were, she would have found herself, metaphorically and vulgarly speaking, up a very fair-sized tree.

"Of course, my dear," continued the Duchess, "I think a certain amount of religion in a country-house is a very good thing, and so I think we'll ask the Bishop of Doncaster."

"Oh no, mamma, pray don't; you'll

have to ask his wife, who hasn't got an 'h' to her back; she was one of his Sunday-school teachers when he was a curate. If you must have a clergyman, try and get Mr. Remarx, he's so interesting; he'll be sure to say all sorts of things to make people talk, and he might preach on Sunday instead of that dreadful Bugsnorter."

"No, dear," replied her Grace, "it's useless to ask Mr. Remarx; he never goes away except into retreat by himself. In fact, I know that at this present time he has gone to a sort of monastery at Malvern, where he is thinking out his sermons for next season; the Marchioness wrote and told me so. No, if we are to go in for the Church, and the Bishop won't do, we'll have the Dean of Dover. He's the wittiest man in England, and has such a dear old face. He has the great advantage of having no vulgar relations. In fact, I believe he's a cousin of the Ormsby Vavasours."

"Well, then, I think we ought to have

a ritualistic lady to counteract those Bramley girls; or, better still, a High Church young man who will shock them. Mr. Denholme will do. He goes to St. Barbara's, and is a member of all sorts of Romish guilds and things."

"He fasts on Fridays, which is rather an objection," said Blanche.

"Oh, never mind that," said the Duchess; "Tissot can easily make up some nice *maigre* dishes for him. I've got a recipe, which was given me by a monk in the south of France, for doing oysters in cream."

In this kind of way, the party for the covert shooting was gradually built up; and in due course they assembled round the hospitable board of Lundy Towers.

The festive week was a time of real hard work for all concerned, hardest, perhaps, for the servants, but nobody thought of them.

The day began somewhere about ten o'clock. A sumptuous breakfast was spread in the green morning-room. It was an unsociable meal, because nobody began quite at the same time as any one else. One had finished his egg before the other had begun his, others had got to the cutlets before a later batch had tackled the fish, the Dean was eating his marmalade, while Mr. Denholme had not poured out the cream into the first of his four cups of tea. This young gentleman seldom got down before 10.20 A.M., though the rule of the Guild of St. Botolph, to which he belonged, suggested 7.30 as the latest hour at which "brothers" should rise. "I got a dispensation from Father Freeborg before I came, you know," he would say in self-defence regularly every morning to the eldest Miss Bramley, who would promptly offer him under the table-cloth a little tract called: "The Jesuits are among us again! Beware!" Published by the "National Society for the Recovery of Reformation Principles." Price 1*d.* for 100.

After breakfast, the shooters departed to the coverts, the ladies, the Dean, Mr.

Denholme, and other half-men sitting in the drawing-room. A good deal of gossip was got through then, though the greater amount was reserved for the hour before evening dinner. Some managed to get a quarter of an hour's walk before luncheon, but this was not *de rigueur*. Luncheon was at 1.30, a very large meal. The Rev. Mr. Bugsnorter, Vicar of the parish of Lundy-cum-Lundy, generally managed to bring some important parochial matter for her Grace's imprimatur at 1.15, which, curiously enough, made it almost necessary for him to stay for lunch. "I hardly like to trespass, your Grace, so soon again upon your Grace's hospitality," he would say, "and moreover, I have left my three boys out in the garden to wait for me, and I think I ought to go to them."

"Oh, bring them in," said the Duchess, resignedly. "I daresay they are hungry after their long walk."

And so they were, poor boys, very hungry indeed, and they did thorough justice to the four courses which regularly succeeded one another at the ducal luncheon-table.

After luncheon, every one assembled round the piano to hear a new duet between Mr. Denholme and Lady Blanche. Mr. Bugsnorter applauded loudly, little suspecting that it was the same duet which the "Sisters Piff Paff" were wont to sing at the "Tivoli." The words, however, were in French, and the old Vicar could hardly be expected to understand. After an impromptu skirt-dance by Lady Blanche, or a reading of one of Ibsen's plays by Mr. Traverdi, an amateur actor, the party would go out for a drive, with the exception of the Bramley girls, who by this time of day had generally got into a state of despair, and walked off by themselves to the neighbouring town to call on the Dissenting minister. Tea was served at five in the pink sitting-room. It was usually at this meal that Miss Georgy Green looked in. She was an old maid, who lived with her sister in the village. Her great delight was to see how the

IN EXCELSIS

upper classes lived, and her "Gleanings from Five-o'clock Tea," had they been published, would have made the fortune of a fashionable bookseller.

"Ah, my love," she would say on her return to the Ivy Cottage, "you should have been there this afternoon; Lady Blanche is getting more amusing every day. I notice, by the way, they don't wear much behind now; I must get my brown silk altered; and the bonnets too are so very small. Then, my love, it's quite wrong to say 'Do you *take* tea?' the Duchess always says simply 'Tea?' It sounds so much better, I think. And then, my dear, we must get into the habit of shaking hands in the right way; you must not do it in a natural kind of way, you must first of all let your right hand hang loosely from your wrist like a drooping lily, then you must raise your arm quite high in the air like you do when the dressmaker measures you round the chest, keeping your right hand drooping all the time, then you must waggle it in your neighbour's eye, and he or she will be ready by this time with his or her right hand in the same kind of position, then you will not grasp it in a vulgar way, but just take his or her third finger between your first and third finger, waggle again, and then it's done."

"Are you quite sure about that, Georgy?" her sister would say.

"Quite sure, my love. I took notes in my pocket-book immediately after I had seen Lady Blanche do it."

Tea was an amusing meal at Lundy, for the guests knew all about Miss Georgy's weaknesses, and behaved in an especially extravagant manner for her benefit. After tea, it being winter-time, there would be a cosy assembly round the large fire in the hall, and a right good gossip until dinner. Dinner was the culmination of all the hopes and anticipations of the day. Even the shooters, engrossed in their sport, had from time to time been looking fondly forward to the evening's rest at the comfortable board, where for two good hours they would graze upon the fat pastures prepared for them by the Duke's Parisian cook.

After dinner, there would be music of a more sedate character than that of the afternoon, there being usually some of the local bigwigs present, who would have been shocked at anything *outré*. At the departure of the bigwigs, however, the fun would become more boisterous. Mr. Trevardi would give an imitation of an Italian prima donna, or the Dean would mesmerise the Duchess. Cards and smoking followed, and it must have been quite two o'clock before the last man turned into bed. It was indeed a hard day's work.

On one day in that week a little variation was caused in the programme owing to a heavy fall of rain. The guests, unable to go out after breakfast, sat in the Hall. It was then that the conversation turned upon the subject of our hero, Stephen Remarx.

It began in this way. Vesey Maitland, who was talking to Lord Arthur, was heard to say, during a lull such as often comes in the midst of a loud conversation, these remarkable words: "I don't think you have any right to retain your shares in the Swampshire Railway Company as long as they treat their men like that."

"What's that?" said the Dean anxiously, for he held a large stake in the Swampshire: "is anything going wrong with the Company?"

"Oh no, don't be afraid, Mr. Dean," replied Lord Arthur, "it's only an absurd idea which Maitland has picked up from that fanatic Remarx, that you ought not to hold shares in a concern where the working-men are not well treated. In the first place, I don't believe the Swampshire men are worse treated than any others. They only work fourteen hours a day." (His Lordship said this with the air of one who had frequently worked as long, and longer himself, though it is needless to observe that, with the exception of making toast for his fagmaster at Eton, he had never done a stroke of manual labour in his life.) "And in the second place, even if they were, I have no right to interfere."

"Not even if you are receiving large dividends from the overwork of these men?" said Maitland. "Supposing one of them died from overwork, would not you have had any part in his death?"

"Of course not: what beastly rot you talk!" said Lord Arthur. "Let's hear your opinion, Mr. Dean."

"Well, of course," said the Dean, cautiously feeling his way, on what he knew to be dangerous ground, "of course, I know that there is a very distinct movement, nowadays, in the direction indicated by my friend, Mr. Maitland, but I think we must be very careful how we proceed. We must always bear in mind that any interference with freedom of contract and the unfettered circulation of capital is likely to land us in a quicksand, whence it will be extremely difficult for us, commercially and industrially speaking of course, to emerge."

A faint murmur of applause greeted this effusion of the Dean's, though nobody knew exactly what he meant.

"But don't you think," ventured Lady Blanche, "that Mr. Remarx must not be taken seriously? I think it was Papa who once said that, if what Remarx suggested in one of his sermons about carrying out the Sermon on the Mount were really done, Society would break up into little pieces in a week."

"I certainly think," continued the Dean, "that some of the things which Mr. Remarx is reported to have said"— ("Some of his 'remarks' in fact," said Mr. Denholme in a childish voice, and then sank back behind a Japanese fan in confusion, nobody having laughed)—"I think that many of these things are purely Utopian: purely Utopian," he repeated, "to the last degree, and in the very worst sense. Moreover, to suppose, that at the end of the nineteenth century of Christianity we are only just finding out, from the lips of a young curate, what religion really is, and what it requires us to do, is absurd, and on the face of it ridiculous."

"And yet," said Maitland,"it was only at the beginning of this same nineteenth century that our forefathers were so ignorant of the principles of Christianity that they quite cheerfully hung people for stealing sheep and even smaller things; and it is only thirty or forty years ago that our fathers complacently allowed children to work in the coal-pits, at the age of six years, without moving a finger to help them; and with all due respect to you, Mr. Dean, even at the end of this nineteenth century I venture to think there's a great deal more for us to learn. Do you think it right, for instance, for nominally Christian landlords to be living in luxurious palaces, while their own tenants are living in unwholesome dwellings which could be pulled down and put up again in a proper way for half the price of what these same men spend on yachting in the Mediterranean?"

The Dean seemed a little confused, but

managed to say: "Well, Mr. Maitland, of course you may look at things in this novel way, and I am an old man, and can't be expected to change now. Of course, I know there's a great deal of poverty in the world, and a great deal of inequality, but it always will be so: 'The poor are always with us,' as the Holy Scriptures say."

"Yes," said Lady Blanche, chiming in with an alarming piece of exegesis, "and it says too that we can 'do what we will with our own;' so why shouldn't we go yachting?"

"Yes," said Lord Arthur, with a crowning misquotation, "and the Catechism says that the poor are to be content, and do their duty in the state of life to which the Almighty has called them."

"What do you think, Miss Bramley?" asked the Dean, hoping to transfer the responsibility of defending the old faith on to younger shoulders.

"Oh, I'm sure I don't know," said Miss Bramley in a rapid voice, and nervously fumbling in her bag for a tract; "I think these things have nothing to do with religion; we've got to save our souls, haven't we? That's the only thing to think about; it's not by works of righteousness that we shall get to Heaven. I don't think Mr. Remarx is a safe guide. I am told he's not converted. I think Mr. Maitland will find out the truth, perhaps, if he reads this." She handed him a large tract on blue paper called "Tares among the Wheat, or the Socialist Satan among the Saints." Then Mr. Denholme, having recovered from his confusion, and thinking that his turn had come, thus delivered himself: "Father Freeborg, you know, whom I look upon as a great authority and a most spiritual man, says that all this Socialism is a great mistake: he thinks that the work of a priest is to deal with heavenly things, and not with dwellings of the poor, and County Councils, and worldly things of that kind. I think he's quite right--don't you? And as for Mr. Remarx, of course he's great fun to listen to. I look upon him as a sort of Church Corney Grain, who does for Sundays, when German Reed's is not open, don't you know? But of course he's not quite Catholic you know, and cne could not make him one's director or anything of that kind, you know."

Then, with a vicious little smile, he walked up to Maitland and said: "My dear Maitland, if you really believe all this nonsense why don't you give up all you possess, and give to the poor, or some equally Quixotic thing of that kind?"

Maitland looked at him sorrowfully and said: "The day may not be so far distant when we shall be called even to that," and he drew from his pocket a small circular, on which were written these words:

Church of St. Mark and the Angels.

Lent Sermons.

The Rector will preach a Course of Sermons, commencing on February 10.

Subject—"*Shall we not follow Christ?*'

IN EXCELSIS

These Sermons are intended for those Christians who wish to take a more definite step towards the imitation of their Master.

IX

THE VENTURE

On February 11, a month after the events described in the last chapter, the following appeared in the *Morning News:*

Extraordinary Sermon at a Chelsea Church.

A great sensation was caused yesterday morning at the Church of St. Mark and the Angels by a sermon preached by the Hon. and Rev. Stephen Remarx, the well-known Rector. The very eccentric doctrines taught by this gentleman have been for some time the talk of London, but a climax was reached yesterday, when he delivered the extravagant discourse of which we give a report below. It is expected that the sermon, which contains the most advanced doctrines of Socialism and Religious Fanaticism, will lead to serious results. In fact, it is reported that the patron, the Marquis of St. Alphege, has already requested Mr. Remarx to resign.

It may interest our readers to recall some facts concerning Mr. Remarx and his family. His brother, the present Earl Remarx, is little known, having resided chiefly abroad, owing to financial difficulties—difficulties which his more fortunate brother does not share, having been well provided for by his father, and having every prospect of succeeding to the vast real and personal property of his uncle the Marquis of St. Alphege, including the mansion in Chelsea Square.

The living of St. Mark's is worth £800 a year, a mere drop in the ocean when compared with the wealth Mr. Remarx already enjoys and will enjoy.

The above was followed by a report of the sermon. But no verbatim report can possibly convey to our readers a true idea of the immense impression produced upon the vast congregation who had assembled to hear the first of Stephen's promised Lenten discourses. Only those who were present could at all appreciate it. Vesey Maitland, who sat in a secluded corner of the gallery and watched the proceedings, has preserved some notes which are here reproduced.

"It was not his eloquence," writes Maitland, "which impressed us all that morning. Stephen was never eloquent, and on that day, perhaps, his words came out less easily than usual. Much of it was just blurted out in a stern voice, though never brutally sarcastic, and always with evident sympathy. He felt intensely all he was saying; it had all been carefully thought out and weighed before he entered the pulpit, yet it was spoken extempore. He held nothing but a New Testament in his hand. He seemed to me to wish every one to feel : 'This message is not mine, but God's ; if I seem to wield a lash, it is for myself to smart as well as you ; I know your difficulties, but I must speak, even if it seem unkind. I can keep it in no longer, the crisis of my ministry has come ; woe is me if I preach not the Gospel.'

The text was from the Sermon on the Mount, always his favourite passage of Scripture, *Ye are the light of the world. A city that is set on a hill cannot be hid.*

He began with a series of almost jerky sentences, roughly put together, and somewhat commonplace.

'Our Lord,' he said, 'in another place calls Himself the Light of the World. He penetrates the soul of each man, lighting up its dark corners, and showing him his sins ; and He shines outside him too, in the darkness of the world, to guide him on his way. But He is also socially the Light of Men, the Light of a Nation, a City, a Society such as this of ours in West London.

'He lights up the life of society, showing it its weaknesses and sins; and then, too, outside He stands, the everlasting Lamp, the perpetual Witness, clear and unmistakable, to show men how they ought to live, bidding them come to Him and walk in the light of His brilliant Presence. Here is the Ideal for every nation, every circle of human beings, to look up to and from which to learn on what principles to act and live.

'But, brethren, He does not say only "I am the Light of the World," but, "*Ye* are the light of the world." We Christians, then, are to act upon the world as our Master does. The Church is to be "a city set on a hill," a compact society of human beings, having in themselves that light-giving power which our Lord Himself has.' Then he plunged into the thick of his message. 'This morning, my friends, I am addressing myself definitely to those who are professing Christians; to those who, outwardly at any rate, belong to that society which our Lord has placed in the world. I am going to ask you some serious questions.

'Are you the light of the world? Your Lord expects it of you. He expects you to be showing an example to the rest of the world. He expects you to be lighting up the darkness, definitely showing this thing and that thing to be evil, and condemning it as such by your words and by your life. He calls on you, in a word, to be separate from the world around you. You are light; the world is dark. You are on a hill; the world is below.

'Let us suppose now that we are worldly people, and let us take our stand and look at these nominal Christians in this London society of ours. Shall we find them so very different from ourselves? Shall we find them standing out, separated from us, so that we feel that we are in the dark and they are in the light—that we are below and they on a hill?'

It was at this point that the congregation seemed to realise that Stephen intended that morning to bring his message home very close to his hearers. It was clear that no rhetoric was to be expected, nothing that they could just admire as a display of genius and then put aside as having no meaning for practical purposes.

'Look at them!' cried Stephen—as if he was really a leader of heathens, wishing to learn by looking at us what true Christianity meant. 'Look at them!' he said, in a voice so earnest that many a man trembled, like Felix of old, at the prospect, of a 'righteousness' about to be revealed.

'Look at them. Some of them are employers of labour—Christians, remember; but what are they doing? Surely they cannot know that those poor girls whom they employ are suffering disease from their neglect; surely they do not know that the conditions under which their workpeople live are such that they can hardly be decent and certainly not happy; surely if they knew it, these "lights of the world," they would try to do something to make things better. Some of them, again, are business men; Christians too, remember, orthodox too, generous perhaps, regular in church; but we follow them on Monday to their offices. We look up to them for light and leading, we poor dark, heathens, who want to know how to live; we find them beggaring their neighbours, we find them not very careful about the strict honesty and fairness of all their dealings. We approach them and ask them if they have forgotten Christ, and they tell us that "business is business," and "religion is only for Sunday." We look again at some grandly dressed people; we remember that we knew them once when they were poor; we wonder how they made their money; we are told it was in trade—in fact, they still draw their wealth from trade. We ask them what sort of trade it is? what effect it has on the lives of others? We ask them whether it is true that the district in the poor part of London where their public-houses chiefly are is well known to be overstocked with such places, and that the population is cursed with drunkenness and misery?

They tell us that they have never inquired about it. We wonder somewhat as we look for light from them.

'Or again, we see some other rich persons who, we are told, possess large shares in several well-known companies. We have heard reports of many grievances which those employed by these companies have got. We ask the shareholders if the grievances are well-founded. They tell us they do not know, and if they did know they could do nothing. We suggest that they might sell out. They stare and laugh, and again we wonder. We turn to another group; this time they are country gentlemen. We have been told that the labourers on their estates are earning a miserable pittance, that they are expected to keep their wives and children every week on exactly the money which these gentlemen spend on two bottles of champagne. We ask them if this is true. They tell us it always has been so, that their fathers went to church and did not think an alteration was necessary, so why should they? We still wait for light.

'Once again, my brethren, we follow that crowd of young men round from church to their club, and we inquire who they are. Six of them are the eldest sons of their parents. We are told they do nothing all day, that they never work because they have no need to do so. We have read somewhere in the Bible that "if any would not work, neither should he eat," and we wonder again as we see them sitting down to lunch.'

Under the excitement of conviction, Stephen had almost forgotten himself—it was the nearest approach to culpable sarcasm in the sermon—if he had gone a step further he would have not only failed of his object by disgusting some of those whose consciences he most wished to quicken, but he would have offended his own sense of humility, which he ever felt most keenly, in the presence of the awful problem. His countenance changed. He paused. He seemed to be casting himself upon God, and saying secretly: "O God, what are we to do? Show us, dear Saviour, how we are to serve Thee! Tell me, now, my Master, what I must tell these people."

Then he began again—

'The light of the world! Is it, then, a sham and a delusion? Are we to despair and say, 'The standard is too high; if Christianity requires so much, we cannot be Christians?' Are we, then, for the most part hypocrites? No, my brothers and sisters, rather we must sit at our Lord's feet again, and hear Him say, 'With men it is impossible, but with God all things are possible.' Then with His help we must set to work to light the lights again. The light has gone out, or it is obscured. It has got mingled with the darkness. We are too much of the world.

'Now, I am not giving you the result of a hasty and superficial survey of the matter, but the result of thought and prayer. Neither do I profess to have found out the answer to all the difficulty. But such as I have I give you.'

Then he unfolded his scheme, without sensation, without emotion, only with a quiet, firm deliberateness, which showed us that he really meant it. Had he spoken now excitedly or with passion, it is possible that hundreds might have been attracted to him for the moment, but the falling away would have been certain and extensive. As it was, a few were drawn, and those most seriously.

'This is my invitation,' he said. 'Some of us must give up all we have. I repeat, we must give up all we have. I do not say that we are to take up our money in a reckless way and throw it into the sea, nor even that we are to give it all to a charitable institution. Rather, we are to take our wealth and lay it at Christ's feet—give it to Him to spend. All of it is to be given to what is right and good.

'There is to be no fanaticism about this, no wild rush into poverty or mendicancy. That will never solve the social problem.

'My idea is, that some few of us might join together and give all our wealth into a common fund to spend for Christ. Wealth, moreover, does not simply mean our ready cash; it means all that wherewith God has endowed us: our intellect, our reason, our powers of mind and hand and heart, our genius, ourselves. All should be massed together and drawn from for the benefit of our fellow-men. We will live together, some of us men, each will give himself for all : the artist will paint for others' joy, the author will write for good, the priest will preach and teach and minister grace; the student will think and read, the politician will use the strength of the Legislature, so far as it will allow him, for the work of Christ and the extension of His kingdom; the poor man who has no t had the advantage of education will join us, to learn maybe, but also to teach us about those with whom he has lived, so that we may all get to know one another as brothers, sons of the One Father. And above all we will study God, we will strive to know what goodness and holiness are, we will read over our Gospels again and learn how to live. Then perhaps we shall be lights.

'Others there might be living more in the world. Many of you have your work, which could not be done under such conditions as these; some of you have homes you could not leave. You I would bid to live in the world, and yet far more strictly than at present, not *of* it. Shun its spirit. Ask not, what do others do? but what does Christ bid *me* do? Look well again at the principles on which you regulate your conduct. Brace them up that they may come nearer to the standard of your Lord; look to your honesty, your purity, your diligence.

'None of us will find it easy. To follow Christ must mean to walk again the way of Calvary. It may mean giving up our friends—many will refuse to walk with us; it may mean giving up our families, turning our backs even on our own flesh and blood. It must mean giving up much comfort and luxury, for a man clothed in soft raiment and living in kings' palaces cannot be a prophet. We shall certainly be spoken against. Woe unto us if we are not! Come out, my brothers, and be separate. "If any man will come after Me, let him deny himself and take up his Cross and follow Me. For whosoever will save his life shall lose it : and whosoever will lose his life for My sake shall find it."

X

SOME PASTORAL EPISTLES

IN order to give a correct version of what passed between Stephen and the Marquis at this eventful period of his career, it is best to reproduce the correspondence itself.

LETTER I.

From the MARQUIS *to* STEPHEN.

DEAR STEPHEN,

The reports which have reached me about your disgraceful behaviour in the pulpit—a pulpit the occupation of which you owe entirely to my liberality,—leave me no alternative but to request you to resign. I know I have no legal power of compelling you to do this, but I put it to your honour—if you have any left. I ask you, therefore to leave the benefice vacant, and to give me the opportunity of placing therein a clergyman whose ideas of what a Christian is will more nearly approach my own. I am writing to the Bishop of London by this post.

Yours affectionately,

SAINT ALPHEGE.

(Dictated.)

P.S.—(*From the Marchioness.*)—I'm awfully sorry about this, Ste, but the Marquis is quite inexorable. I think if you were to apologise and promise not to be quite so *prononcé* again, he would cave in. Do take care of yourself, and don't do anything foolish with this new plan of yours.

AUNT ALF.

LETTER II.

From the MARQUIS *to the* BISHOP.

MY DEAR LORD BISHOP,

Reports may have already reached your Lordship of the very disgraceful conduct of my misguided nephew, the Rector of St. Mark and the Angels. I have been told that he preached a sermon in which Socialism, Radicalism, Anarchism, and every conceivable abomination were freely advocated. He proposes to form some kind of society for the propagation of these dangerous principles, a course which I have no doubt your Lordship will agree with me would imperil the very existence of the Established Church, and which I hope your Lordship will absolutely forbid him to pursue. I have written to Mr. Remarx, requesting him, as a personal favour to me and to prevent any unpleasantness, to resign the living. I shall request your Lordship to institute the Rev. Amos Bugsnorter to the living, who is at present the Duke of Lundy's clergyman, a most earnest man, and one in every way likely to restore this unhappy parish to a state of peace and quietness after this unfortunate disturbance.

I am, my Lord,
Yours faithfully
Saint Alphege.

(Dictated.)

Letter III.

From the Hon. and Rev. Stephen Remarx *to his* Uncle.

Dear Uncle St. Alphege,

I beg to acknowledge your letter, and to say that I already meditated doing what you have asked me to do. I have for some time felt that the particular line of conduct which I am trying to follow will make it difficult for me to give sufficient attention to the proper working of this enormous parish. I therefore beg to tender my resignation of the benefice of St. Mark and the Angels. May I, however, request as a great favour, that you will appoint as my successor one who will continue the many organisations for the relief of the poor, etc., which I have, by God's help, been allowed to start in the parish during my incumbency.

Yours truly,

STEPHEN REMARX.

P.S.—I think I should be shrinking from my duty as a Christian minister were I not to point out to you that your conduct towards me is not in accordance with your profession as a Christian. If at any time you would wish to see me, and to let me help you to follow out your professed religion more effectually, I shall be glad to call.

S. R.

XI

PROGRESS

THE London season was over. The Park was nearly empty. On a seat near the Achilles statue sat Paul Durnford and John Oxenham. Our friend Paul had only that afternoon returned from a journey on the Continent, whither he had been sent by his Library Commissioners on literary business.

"And now that we are seated, John, tell me how it's all going on," said Paul. "I have been out of everything. With the exception of a curiously garbled version of the celebrated sermon in *Galignani*, and a rambling account of the new society which was given me by a Roman Catholic student at St. Cyr called Denholme, I have really heard nothing about it. First of all, tell me, how is our dear Stephen."

"Oh, he's first-rate, only a little tired after all the bother of getting us fairly launched; but, please God, we are all going for a little rest to the sea soon," said John.

"How many are there of you?" asked Paul.

"Only six at present of the 'regulars.' You will make the seventh of course, and then there are some hundreds of the other kind; but I had better explain. First of all, you must know that almost immediately after Stephen had delivered his sermon, the Marquis of St. Alphege called upon him to resign, which he did. St. Mark's Church was given to an old clergyman called Bugsnorter, who managed in three Sundays to almost completely empty it. On the third Sunday of his incumbency he delivered his sermon to his family (who occupied, I think, three pews), and the Bible-woman.

But I must tell you about Stephen. For the first few days after the sermon he was beset by every kind of person. Newspaper interviewers came in crowds, but were never suffered to pass the threshold. Nevertheless, the *Piccadilly Gazette* managed to fill two columns with a 'Chat with John the Baptist,' while the *Monthly of Monthlies* gave a 'Character Sketch,' which revealed the fact that the editor had known Stephen from his childhood, and had practically inspired him with all his ideas. I don't think Stephen minded the papers much, except perhaps the report in the *Meteor*, which pained him. It was headed: 'Chucked out of Chelsea. The Parson and the Peer. Parson Remarx passes remarks. The Marquis does not like it, and chucks him out of a fat living.' Then there must have been at least 300 people who came and offered to belong to the Society whenever it should be formed. This proves, what at one time I should have doubted, that there are very large numbers of rich people who are anxious to serve Our Lord and His poor, and who only want to be shewn the way. Yes, Durnford, if I had my life over again

I would cut out my tongue rather than talk against the rich as I used to do. Often and often have I borne false witness against my neighbour. The truth is, we are all the same, poor and rich, very feeble imitators of Our Master. Henceforth let us lay aside mutual recriminations and work together for the common good. Yet we only have six members at present. This fact alone will show you how strict Stephen has been. It is the poverty which chokes them off. Nobody is allowed to possess a penny. All our money is in one common fund, and it is dealt with only at the will of the six members, who meet together every day to settle what to do. About half is sent to home and foreign missions, and the rest is spent on our work. As you may imagine, I did not contribute much, but I am giving myself and all my energy to the work, and I can tell you it's much harder than dock labour. Others of us, of course, contributed large sums. Stephen himself was rich, and so was Maitland.

He is the Radical M.P. for one of the East-end districts, but he lives with us, going down to the House every day during the session. He has been doing splendid work with the new Factory Bill this last session. He had a large estate in Wiltshire, and he was doubtful for a time whether he ought not to go and look after it, but eventually he thought it best to sell it to a Christian purchaser, one of the 'irregular army,' as we call them, Lord Mount Pleasant.

"The other three of us are the Duke of Dalston, Frank Newton, and Doctor Probyn. The Duke has sold all his possessions, and has made over his London property to his mother. He was able to effect this transaction because his father died just before he came of age, and he had a free hand to do as he liked with the estate. We look after the houses, and see that they are all as they should be, and the rents are collected by us for the Duchess.

"Frank is the sweetest person in the

world. He is a painter. To look at him is to know what love is. The work he is doing down in South London for churches and schools and the people's homes is quite wonderful. You may ask, perhaps, what he has given up for Christ. He has given up the prospect of being one of the greatest men of our time in a worldly sense. He would probably have been an A.R.A. next year, and as he is only nineteen years old, you can see that he was on the way to what men call greatness.

"Then there is Doctor Probyn. You know his name, I suppose. He was the fashionable physician. Now we call him Luke. His practice is now entirely in the slums. The money he earns goes, of course, into our fund.

"Now, I must tell you of a most important thing that happened within a few weeks of our start. The Marquis of St. Alphege died. By his will it was found that he had deprived Stephen of almost everything, and had left it to his grand nephew, who lives in Manitoba. Curiously, however, he left Stephen the big house. Stephen believes that this piece of generosity was due to the entreaties of his aunt, the Marchioness, who I must tell you has become an altered woman now, and is one of the 'irregulars.'

"The house was, of course, just what we wanted. The property would have been an encumbrance. It is in this house we live. Fancy my living in a lord's Westend mansion! But it is not much like a mansion now.

"We six live in the top part of the house, in what used to be the servants' bedrooms. We have one room each, no carpet, no curtains, and a simple little bed. The whole of the rest of the house, with the exception of some spare rooms which we are keeping unfurnished, is given to the people. The large drawing-rooms are still kept as reception-rooms. Here we hold our parties twice a week. Anyone can come: rich and poor meet together.

"What wonderful transactions take place

there week by week! Only last night there was the Earl of Cumborough making up a beautiful little arrangement with that clever Jack Burdon, the pupil teacher, to pay for the whole of his education at Oxford; while Lady Merthyr was organising a visit of the factory girls to Merthyr Castle for three weeks in September. The other rooms are used for all kinds of purposes. The 'irregulars' come and work there of an evening, some holding classes, some just reading a book with the men and boys. The library is still used for its original purpose, or rather it now fulfils its purpose, which it never did before. I sometimes wonder what the old Marquis would say if he came back to life and saw our young men sitting in his library and reading his books.

"The coach-house is used as a gymnasium, and the kitchen for cookery classes. The billiard-room and conservatory, at the end of the garden, which form a separate house, is now our hospital, where Dr.

Probyn looks after his little ones. Two sisters of charity live there to attend to the sick children. I must not forget the chapel, where every day we receive the Sacrament, and where for an hour each morning Stephen expounds to us the Gospel."

"'Tell me something more about the 'irregular' army," said Paul Durnford.

"Well," said Oxenham, "they number about two hundred and fifty. They belong to every class and profession. You would hardly believe it, but Joe Binks is one of them. Dr. Probyn saved his wife's life, and that was too much for Joe. She was more precious to him than Cain's wife, and he gave up Bible smashing, and became a Christian, and a thorough one too. Then there are lawyers and stockbrokers, doctors and soldiers; any one, in fact, who will solemnly promise to keep Christ's law in the midst of this wicked world, and to do some practical work for his fellow-men. We've got some of those poor eldest sons among them, and they are doing their best, though it's very hard. Three of them are going to look after our boys at Clovelly next month, instead of shooting grouse; and if that's not religion, I don't know what is."

"Have you any definite rule for them? How do you keep them in continuous touch with your work?" asked Paul.

"They are bound by one rule besides the promises, and that is, to stay at least a fortnight with us during the year. During that time they will talk matters over with us and we shall give each other advice as to how to act in a Christian way in the world, and how to spend money in the best way."

"But," said Paul, "do not some of them find it very difficult to keep their promises."

"Very difficult indeed," said Oxenham. "A country gentleman who fills his house with university extension students instead of partridge shooters finds himself cut by the county; a fishmonger who has begun to tell the truth about the freshness of his fish to his customers has lost half his custom: a pawnbroker, too, has found his profits declining because he has been giving people the true value of the goods which they bring to pledge. But the best case of all is that of Mr. Dyvese, a brother of the late Sir Henry, whom he succeeded as Chairman of the Match Company. He is one of our 'irregulars,' and he went on in such a way about the poor girls that he was called upon to resign, and he did so."

"Do you find that many of the 'irregulars' give it up after a bit?"

"Yes," said Oxenham, "a few do. Lady Sapphira, a married lady, began well, but she hardly caught the spirit of the thing, and gave it up. Sir Simon Maggs, too, was a great one at it for a short time, but we found he wanted to make it a commercial concern, and so we were obliged to tell him that he must go."

"Is it too soon, John, to say if any effect

is being produced on society at large by what you are doing?" asked Durnford.

"My dear Durnford," said Oxenham, "I don't altogether like your question; in fact, it is against our rules to trouble ourselves about results. We must be content to go on until we die, even if nothing substantial seems to come of it. Think of the Master dying on the Cross, deserted by all His friends and seemingly a failure. This much I will say because He has told us not to be surprised if the world hates us. We are awfully hated. I believe there are some who would almost kill us if they dared. I am told that things have been said against us in ballrooms and at dinner parties. I have heard people laughing at us as we walk along the street, and on two occasions men spat in Stephen's face. But we take no notice. Neither do we attempt to answer the misrepresentation of the Press. At first the papers looked upon us as material for sensational 'copy.' That passed off, and then began a 'correspondence.' We have been described as Lunatics, Jesuits, Jumpers, Vagabonds, and Anarchists, but we never reply. No, we go on silently. It is better. Besides, it is more like Christ."

XII

JUDGMENT

STEPHEN and his friends did not call their Society by any name.

Accordingly, Mr. Whittaker was not able to secure for them a place among his 250 different sects side by side with the Quakers and the followers of Johanna Southcott. In "high society" they were known as the "Remarkables," and many a wild rumour went round concerning them. At a Foreign Office "crush" you might hear some languid "Johnnie" saying to a fair *débutante:* "I say, Miss ——, have you heard the latest about those 'Remarkables'? They feed on fourpence a day and flog each other every morning. 'Pon my word, I've a good mind to join them myself, if only to save my bills, though I should not like the cat o' nine tails." "Oh! fancy you, Mr. —— in a long cloak like Mr. Remarx—oh! how funny!" Or one might hear an old dowager lamenting the new departure in religion to her companion on the sofa: "I call it flying in the face of Providence to go out of the world like that. Surely the good gifts of the earth were meant to be enjoyed. To think of that dear Duke of Dalston giving up all his possessions— it's a blasphemy, that's what it is. And as for that 'irregular army' or whatever they call themselves, I think they are the worst of the lot. They're a positive nuisance, interfering with their absurd maxims and precepts every five minutes. Lent sermons at St. Paul's, Knightsbridge, are bad enough for six weeks; but when it comes to 'You must not do this,' and 'You must not do that,' all the year round, it's cruel. Besides, I think it's most improper to have religion introduced at a dinner-table. The other day I was dining at the Duchess of Lundy's, and

JUDGMENT

there were no less than six of these eccentric creatures there, and their carryings-on were simply scandalous. One man went on saying his grace a long time after the Duke had finished it. You know the beautiful way the Duke says grace. He just says 'Praised' and then we all begin dessert. And then none of these goody-goodies would laugh when the Duchess told that exceedingly funny story of the Manners-Gigby divorce case. I call it so rude not to laugh at your hostess' stories. And then one of them actually had the effrontery to tell somebody point-blank to his face that some of the words he used were not fit to be spoken by a Christian. Really, Society will be unbearable if this kind of thing is allowed to go on much longer. I wish somebody would speak to the Bishop of London, or the Lord Chamberlain, or some one of that kind, and get it put down."

The following report of the first chapter meeting of the whole Society, held within a year from its foundation, will convey a good idea of the progress of its work and the difficulties it has had to contend with. The report is written by Frank Newton the artist, and is contained in a private manuscript which was not originally intended for publication. I am, unfortunately, not able to reproduce the pen and ink illustrations which adorn the report. Some of them are extremely clever, notably the frontispiece, which I think is intended to depict the triumph of Religion over Belgravia.

Extracts from Frank's Report.

"Stephen is in the chair. Over his head hangs that sweet picture, 'Come unto Me.' We have said our prayers. Shall I ever forget that 'Veni Creator,' that 'Magnificat,' that Creed, or that 'Our Father,' rising like a great battle-cry to God? As we said 'Thy will be done on earth as it is in Heaven,' it seemed to me that sympathetic seraphs filled the room and sang 'Amen.'

JUDGMENT

"Then each of the brothers and sisters gave testimony and experience of living the Christian life in the midst of the world. First came the clergy. Their chief enemies seemed to be their relations and their Squires. 'I never quite knew before,' said one priest, 'why it might be necessary to hate one's father and mother. Since I began to lead a poor life, sharing my dinner often with those who are badly off, I have had nothing but furious persecution from my relations. I am told that I am mad, and fit only to be shut up in an asylum. In fact, I have found it necessary to keep from going to my home in order to avoid quarrels. My Squire, too, has withdrawn all his subscriptions from the church because I was present at a meeting of the Agricultural Labourers' Union, and spoke in favour of an attempt to call attention to their crying grievances, and also because I lent the National schoolroom to the Gladstonian candidate, and asked him to remove his high pew, which he seldom uses, in order to make room for some more seats for the poor.' The poor town clergy seemed to have fared no better. One of them read out some letters which he had received from old supporters who had withdrawn their aid because of his attitude towards the Women Workers' movement. 'You seem to me,' wrote one of his correspondents, 'to completely misunderstand your duties as a minister. You have no concern whatever with these matters. Your business is to lead men to be content with their wages, and to look forward to a brighter land hereafter.'

"The next to render their account were the professional men. The lawyers seemed to be getting on happily, but the stockbrokers were in despair. Their life in the light of an earnest following of Christ appeared to be made up of ghastly fictions and unreal bargaining. Three of them expressed their wish to leave their occupation and to take to something else. The doctors and dentists, singers and actors, too, seemed uneasy about the fees, and Stephen was asked to appoint a sub-committee to inquire into the ethics of proportionate reward. Then came the business men. One aged employer gave us a simple and humble account of how he had six months before, for the first time in his life, taken the trouble to visit and to get to know those who worked for him. The revelations of the life that some of them led had induced him to completely change the conduct of the trade. He was rebuilding the workshops and providing every facility for the health and happiness of his people. They were allowed a time for recreation every day, and he closed early twice a week. Gymnasia had been erected for the boys and girls, and reading-rooms for all. He had never realised before that drawing-rooms were desirable for any but the upper and middle classes. Every single man, woman and child in his employ was now received at his private house, and they were fast making real friends with his own family. The profits of the business had gone down three per cent., and he had had to refuse to give his daughter a grand piano for her wedding present; but he thanked God all the same.

"Other employers gave similar testimony. Many, too, showed how by 'conciliation' they were warding off labour troubles among their men, and were getting to know them and understand them better.

"The tradesmen came next, with an appalling exposure of the 'tricks of the trade.' They told how the sugar and tea were adulterated, the milk starched, the cloth shoddied, the butter larded, the beer watered (and worse), the coffee chicoried, and the houses jerry-built. They told how the girls were bullied and the boys made to tell falsehoods and cheat with the weights; they told how the women were 'sweated' and underpaid. All this and much more that was sinful they had sworn to give up for Christ's sake; and now, in a purer atmosphere and with cleaner hands, though perhaps with declining profits, they, too, thanked God.

"The rest told like tales of brave renunciations and open confessions of Christ before men. The country gentlemen spoke of cottages rebuilt, and allotments let, and village clubs organised, and drawing-rooms and dining-rooms opened to the poor, and comforts for the aged. The young men told how they had learnt to work for others' good and to despise an idle day."

"Then Stephen rose to make his final speech, of which these are only some notes:

"'Dear sisters and brothers in the Lord, I do thank our God and Father for what we have heard to-day. Yours are brave lives, braver and harder than those which we live here in Alphege House. We have our temptations it is true, but they are not so terrible as yours. Let me comfort you with the words of our adorable Master: "Marvel not my brethren if the world hate you. Ye know that it hated Me before it hated you. Blessed are ye when men shall hate you, and when they shall separate you from their company, and shall reproach you, and cast out your name as evil, for the Son of Man's sake. Rejoice ye in that day and leap for joy." Yes, you are treading where the saints have trod. Only remember, your lives will not get easier as time goes on. It is an uphill path, the path to the Cross. The world will go on scoffing, the suffering will increase. But take it up, offer it a willing sacrifice to Him who made you. Possibly it might be better if some of you were to join your lives and works together. If, for example, you employers who are Christians would give employment to others who want to live a good life too ; if some of these poor persecuted boys and girls could work for you, you would help each other to be Christ-like. In this way the Church would become more in reality what she is in theory, the home of Christ-loving people, the refuge from the storms of

JUDGMENT

Satan, founded on the "Rock of Ages."

"'Never forget that the motto of our brotherhood is "Be ye followers of Christ." We know not what misfortunes may be coming upon us. This may be the last time we shall meet together in this world. But go bravely on. If any fall away, do not despair. Remain firm, if only a few are left. The Lord be with you.'

"This is all I can remember of what he said, but his face—I see it still: it shone like the face of an angel.

"FRANK NEWTON."

XIII

ON THE FEAST OF STEPHEN

It was a Christmas night of the old-fashioned type. London was wrapped in snow. Few people were in the streets, for all who were able were wisely occupied indoors with snapdragon, mistletoe, holly, and mince-pies. Poor old Snivel was trudging along the Thames Embankment. He had left his home in the Borough, where poor little Kittie lay sick, that he might try and pick up a few coppers round the big hotels at Charing Cross. "There's a gran' ball on to night at the 'Cosmopolly,'" his wife had told him. She had heard it from Tim Tittles the crossing-sweeper. "Maybe you'll get summut for callin' the nobses' cabs." So the poor old fellow had put on his crazy hat and

ON THE FEAST OF STEPHEN

sallied forth. He was seventy-nine years old; he had no shirt; all he could call his own was his chronic asthma and the "brownkiters."

Sir Humphrey Juniper had been born on the same day as old Snivel, nine-and-seventy years before, and he had chronic asthma too, but on that Christmas night he was safely ensconced in his villa at Monaco. There was no snow to bother him, and no sick grand-daughter to worry him, and every prospect of plenty for breakfast next morning. And yet he was not really as happy as the old Borough "cad;" for Sir Humphrey had a pricking conscience. He had that morning refused to help his widowed sister, whose sons were a trouble to her. She had written to ask for a little Christmas box and the Baronet had answered "No."

Ah, yes, old Snivel was the happier, in spite of the snow, as he walked to Charing Cross.

"I must go and listen to the Sisters before I go to my work," said the old man to himself. It was his little bit of seasonable pleasure. For the last three Christmases he had stood outside the "Hostel of the Holy Child" and listened to the Sister as they chanted their night office. "Ain't it just nice?" he asked himself as he leant against the lamp-post while the hymn was wafted out to him on the crisp, cold air:

> "Come and behold Him, born the King of Angels;
> Oh come ye, oh come ye to Bethlehem."

"I'd like to go to Bethlem," said the old man. 'Oh my! ain't it cold? I'd like to see that Child they talk of. I s'pose that's his picture," he said faintly as he looked up at the gateway of the Hostel, on which was sculptured the baby face of the King of Kings in His holy mother's arms. "I wish, I wish I could see that Child." And then old Snivel tottered and fell into the arms of a man in a black cloak.

"Hold my stick, Vesey," said Stephen, "or I shall drop him. He'll soon be all right. It's only the cold. Why, look at the poor old chap, he has got no shirt on. A nice sort of Christmas he's having."

Maitland and Stephen Remarx (for it was they who rescued Snivel) were returning from a visit to Rotherhithe. They had been spending the day and night previous in a pestilential slum in that neighbourhood, where the influenza was raging. They were both thoroughly tired out, especially Stephen, and were looking forward with almost boyish delight to a late Christmas supper at Alphege House. But it was not to be. "Frank and Jack, the Doctor and the Duke, will have to wait," said Stephen. "We must take the old man home."

"Where do you live?" said Vesey, for Snivel had come to himself by this time.

"Padarice Terrus," he replied, "in the Burrer."

"Paradise I suppose he means," said Stephen. "I wonder who the fiend was who called all these dreadful places by such pretty names. All right, old man, I know where it is. We'll take you home.

I'm sorry we can't call a cab, but we've got no money; so we'll carry you."

"Be you from Bethlem?" said the old man, his mind still running on the hymn.

"No, from Rotherhithe," said Stephen, smiling. "But come along, it's striking twelve by Big Ben, and we must get to Paradise to-day. Here, put my cloak round him, Vesey."

So they took him home.

There was Christmas joy that midnight after all in Paradise Terrace. If he did not see the Child Himself, the old man saw something very much like Him in those two friends, the parson and the Member of Parliament.

Poor little Kitty almost revived at the sight of the kindness her grandfather was receiving.

"We'll take you in the morning to our Children's Hospital," said Stephen; "good Doctor Probyn will come and fetch you. And you two old people," he continued, turning to Snivel and his wife, "you must live here no longer; you are past work, and I know you don't want to go to the 'House'; but I have got a kind lady who has just opened an Almshouse, a real 'Paradise Terrace' down in Kent. She will take you in next week, and meantime we'll make you comfortable. Wait a minute—I'll be back directly." And Stephen slammed the creaking door behind him.

A quarter of an hour later he returned. "Here, missus," he said, "here's ninepence to get your breakfast with."

"Hullo, Stephen, where did you get that from?" asked Vesey in surprise.

"Never you mind," said Stephen; and then in a whisper he added: "I knocked up old Cheetham, a relation of mine, and he gave me ninepence on my shirt and waistcoat."

"But, my dear fellow, you'll be so cold."

"Never mind," said Stephen, though he shivered as he spoke. "I have got my cloak, and besides, if old Snivel can do without a shirt, why can't I? Come along, V., we'll soon be home."

They hurried over Blackfriars Bridge as the cathedral clock struck four.

* * * *

The last of the dancers was at that moment bidding "Good-bye" to his hosts at the "Hotel Cosmopole."

"A rippin' good ball I call it, old chappy. Ta, ta, Harry! Ta, ta, Arthur!"

It was Captain Deadly who spoke, and our old friends Lord Arthur and Lord Henry who answered "Good-bye."

"I say it's quite hot in here," said Lord Arthur, "in spite of the cold outside. Let's open the window in the supper-room and sit there a bit before we turn in, Harry."

"By George, I wouldn't care to sleep out there to-night," said Henry, looking towards the Embankment.

"Oh that's all rot," said Arthur. "It was only old Booth, who had a nightmare and thought he saw some poor devils out on the riverside; but it wasn't true—at least the papers said not."

"I'm not so sure about that" said Henry, dubiously.

"Well, I'm blowed!" said Lord Arthur,

with an oath, suddenly. " Do you see those two fellows coming along there by the lamp-post? Now, I'll eat my hat if they aren't that canting idiot, Remarx, and that beast, Maitland."

"Are you sure?" said Henry.

"Yes; I should know them a mile off. Look—they're by the lamp now. Yes, it is they. You cursed, canting——"

"Don't talk like that, Arthur," remonstrated Henry.

"I'll just remind them of my presence, though," said Arthur, gathering up some snow from the window-sill. "Look here, Harry, be sure and shut it down directly I've shied this. Here goes!"

Blinded for the moment, and losing his balance, Stephen fell into the roadway. A shout from the driver of a cart rang out on the still morning air. It was too late. The wheel went over him.

* * * *

"It's a cruel business," said Doctor Probyn an hour later, as he sat by the bedside of the unconscious Stephen in the "Hostel of the Holy Child."

They were kneeling round his bed, those six men who had followed him, and with him had found their Lord. Who can describe the cloud of dark sadness that was then descending upon their loving hearts, as it became only too evident that Stephen had received a fatal injury. The earnest face of Oxenham was turned towards him. Tears trickled down his firm and manly countenance. He could not speak: he could only gaze, and think of all that he owed of life and light to that poor sufferer upon the bed. Ah what a debt it was! All the inspiration of his life, all that new vigour that had lately come into his work for humanity, all that hope for the present and future of God's earth and people, all that intense insight into the importance and reality and issues and meanings of things which comes from faith in the Incarnation of the Son of God—all this he owed to Stephen. And then for Paul Durnford, what an awful hour was this! Was he really going to be bereft of that presence which since the old Oxford days had

ON THE FEAST OF STEPHEN

been his greatest joy and strength? He thought of a day some ten years back when, in Magdalen Gardens, Stephen had walked with him and spoken of the Deity of Christ. Paul at that time was afflicted with doubts and difficulties, and it was his friend who had brought him out of darkness into light. He had fought his way through mists and fogs to the day of faith, and it was Stephen who had been his leader under God.

Or Maitland, or Frank, or the Duke—what of them? Each in his different way had been brought under the influence of this strangely holy man. Each had learnt something from his wonderful enthusiasm; each had caught something of his genius for self-sacrifice. And the Doctor too: he thought of a former occasion on which he had stood by Stephen's sick-bed, and in the contemplation of his superhuman patience and perfect self-control in agony had learnt that something of the heroism of Calvary may still be reproduced in Christ's own soldiers who believe in Him.

My God, my God!" said Vesey on

his knees, "if only for one moment, let him speak to us. I cannot, I dare not live without him. Stephen," cried the poor fellow in his anguish, "Stephen, my brother, my dearest, dearest brother!"

There was an awful silence, broken only by the fitful breathing of the dying priest.

"Open the door," said the Doctor; "he wants air."

"Will the music disturb him?" whispered the Sister; "they are singing the Eucharist in the chapel."

"No," said Doctor Probyn, "he has almost joined the Choir."

She opened the door, and there arose from the chapel below the soothing monotone of the Day's Epistle:

"And they stoned Stephen, calling upon God, and saying: 'Lord Jesus, receive my spirit.' And he kneeled down, and cried with a loud voice: 'Lord, lay not this sin to their charge.' And when he had said this, he fell asleep."

www.ingramcontent.com/pod-product-compliance
Lightning Source LLC
Chambersburg PA
CBHW030333170426
43202CB00010B/1116